MY TRIP TO
HEAVEN

Books by David E. Taylor

Face-to-Face Appearances from Jesus

Available From Destiny Image Publishers

MY TRIP TO

HEAVEN

FACE TO FACE WITH JESUS

David E. Taylor

DESTINY IMAGE® PUBLISHERS, INC.

P.O. Box 310, Shippensburg, PA 17257-0310

"Speaking to the Purposes of God for This Generation and for the Generations to Come."

This book and all other Destiny Image, Revival Press, MercyPlace, Fresh Bread, Destiny Image Fiction, and Treasure House books are available at Christian bookstores and distributors worldwide.

For a U.S. bookstore nearest you, call **1-800-722-6774.**

For more information on foreign distributors, call **717-532-3040.**

Reach us on the Internet: **www.destinyimage.com.**

Trade Paper ISBN 978-0-7684-3654-9

Hardcover ISBN 978-0-7684-3655-6

Large Print ISBN 978-0-7684-3656-3

Ebook ISBN 978-0-7684-9036-7

For Worldwide Distribution, Printed in the U.S.A.

1 2 3 4 5 6 7 8 / 14 13 12 11

DEDICATION

To Father God, Jehovah, who revealed His Son Jesus to me at the age of 17 by allowing Him to appear to me. I thank you! And to Jesus, my King and best friend, who is the very reason for my being, and who has stood with me through the darkest times of my life. To the person of the Holy Spirit, who is also my Friend and closest Companion while here on earth.

ACKNOWLEDGMENT

To Jesus, my inspiration.

CONTENTS

PREFACE

THIS BOOK IS a sequel to my first book, *The Ultimate Intimacy: Face-to-Face Appearances from Jesus*. To get the full impact of this book, I highly recommend that you also read the first book as it lays the foundation for many of the things I share in this sequel. Many who read my first book have already begun to have face-to-face visitations from Jesus. Men and women, including pastors, ministers, and business people who had never seen Jesus, have experienced their first appearance from Christ. In the first book, I share how Jesus initially appeared to me when I was just 17 years of age. I was unsaved and in the world, smoking dope, in a gang, and living a riotous life. In both books I followed the leading of the Spirit and decided to share these appearances out of sequential order so that they would be easy to understand and follow.

In this book, I share many of the glories that I saw and experienced as I was taken out of my body and to Heaven by the Lord Jesus Christ. Every time I read this book, I relive those glorious experiences as Christ toured me around Heaven. I also share trips to hell that Jesus took me on and the warnings I learned from them. This book is different from many on this subject of seeing Jesus face to face as I really emphasize relationship and intimacy with Christ. There are three books I've read about people's face-to-face visitations with Jesus and their encounters with the Father in the throne room that have become my favorites: Jesse Duplantis' *Heaven, Close Encounters of the God Kind*; Mary K. Baxter's account of visiting hell entitled, *A Divine Revelation of Hell*; and Rick Joyner's, *The Final Quest*. There are others that include Choo Thomas' book entitled, *Heaven Is So Real* and *23 Minutes in Hell* by Bill Wiese. But the first three that I mentioned have been the most inspirational to me. The point that the Lord instructed me to make here is that most of the experiences these men and women have had from the Lord were concerning God-given appointments and assignments. These experiences seem to have been given to them concerning their ministry to the body and not necessarily strictly because of intimacy.

Although face-to-face visitations with Jesus are part of His purpose and assignment to reach the church and the world, the Lord prizes intimacy more than anything! This was Christ's whole reason for coming to earth—to reconcile us to God and to restore an intimacy with Him that was once lost. It is not about a one-time, face-to-face experience with Jesus or the Father, because the Lord wants you to enjoy a lifetime of intimate relationship with Him. This book is a record of 20 years of continual, face-to-face appearances from the Lord Jesus Christ and multiple visits to the throne room in Heaven to see God the Father Himself. I have experienced this type of relationship with God up until this very day, and you can have it too. This book is not simply an invitation to a one-time encounter, but an invitation into an intimate relationship with Him.

In my first book, I shared about God's love, as it was revealed through His compassion and mercy in our face-to-face relationship. But in this sequel, I not only share my trip to Heaven with you, but I also explain the maturing process that Jesus took me through so that He could personally introduce me as a "Son of God" to His Father, Jehovah God, and to prepare me to work with Him one-on-one in ministry on the earth. Some of the things I write may sound a little difficult for some of you. What I mean specifically is that in this book I talk about the other side of God's love, which the church so desperately needs to hear about and receive because it creates new avenues to walk into higher realms with God and a greater level of intimacy with Christ. God's love is also revealed to us through chastisement.

> *Blessed is the man whom thou chastenest...* (Psalm 94:12).

> *For whom the Lord loveth he chasteneth, and scourgeth every son whom he receiveth. If ye endure chastening, God dealeth with you as with sons* (Hebrews 12:6-7).

If you ever want to have a relationship with God the Father, and not just Jesus, you must go through His discipline process. The joys and rewards of this process lead into the ultimate intimacy that I only just began to talk to you about in the first book. This ultimate intimacy is only just beginning when Christ starts appearing to you. It is wonderful when Jesus appears to you face to face, but there's more. It is Jesus' assignment and ministry to reconcile and introduce us to God the Father. He came to restore our access to the Father, which we had lost through our sins. This is the greatest level and the highest glory. It is not meeting Jesus face to face, but being introduced by Jesus to Jehovah God in a personal way since He is both Jesus' Father and our Father.

> *...neither knoweth any man the Father, save the Son, and he to whomsoever the Son will reveal him* (Matthew 11:27).

The ultimate intimacy is not just knowing Jesus only but also God the Father who sent Him. Jesus Himself stated this in John 17:3:

And this is life eternal, that they might know thee the only true God, and Jesus Christ, whom thou hast sent (John 17:3).

And Jesus is the only One who can bring you into this face to face relationship with God.

...no man cometh unto the Father, but by me (John 14:6).

The Lord Jesus Christ can also take you to Heaven just as He took the prophets and the men and women of old to meet with the Father at the throne of God. Through the testimonies I share and the teachings I give in this book and in my first, the Lord has been appearing to thousands and has taken them on glorious trips to Heaven. We've already heard amazing reports!

Buckle up, stay seated, and expect great things as you experience this glorious trip to Heaven that the Lord will take you on!

Chapter 1

FACE-TO-FACE DISCIPLESHIP:

"The Special Training From the Face of Jesus
Through Appearances Begins"

Becoming His Personal Disciple

THE LORD FIRST appeared to me and began discipling me at the early age of 17 years old. I didn't realize at the time that He was personally discipling me, but in this visitation He told me to forsake my best friend and follow Him. He personally discipled me for a year until I was 18 years old at which time He commissioned me as His servant to preach the gospel. At the age of 19, He tested my walk of faith and started calling me His friend. The Lord wanted to know if I would be obedient and give up my career and home to follow Him wherever He commanded me to go. I obeyed.

After I first obeyed His call, I noticed that the nature of the visitations changed, and that the Lord started calling me His friend in front of others in these visitations. I didn't know at the age of 19 that I had fulfilled His requirements of obedience. I just loved Him, and I didn't have revelation of what was really happening to me like I do today! At 19 years old, I had only been walking with the Lord for three years, and I had already passed this test of obedience and faith in the same way that Abraham was tested. God asked me to do what He commanded me to do without any money and I did it. I just believed Him! I didn't know or understand the significance of this at the time, but years later He revealed to me that I became His personal pupil, student, and disciple at the very beginning of my walk. He required me to give up everything—my career and the city where I grew up and lived—and to follow Him on nothing but faith! I began obeying His command to love Him more than my parents, my best friend, and even my own life. I didn't realize at the time that He put me at the discipleship level with Him when I had my first open vision and stood face to face with Jesus. After my obedience had been tested, the visitations changed. I started having face-to-face encounters with the Lord where He taught me directly and trained me through discipline.

Being Jesus' Personal One-on-One Disciple or Student

How to Become a Personal Disciple of Jesus

Being Trained by Jesus Personally

I didn't realize it, but I had become Jesus' personal disciple because I had given up everything to follow Him. He visited me again around this time and told me to walk in the same type of faith that Abraham had walked in, forsaking everything to follow the Lord wherever He led me. This meant I became His personal student, which in turn meant that He became my personal teacher and trainer.

This word *disciple* is in the same family of the word *discipline* that comes from the Greek word *mathetas* which means "a learner, pupil, someone enrolled as a scholar to be instructed or to be trained."[1] Sometimes training requires (if we are truly to follow Him) that the Lord not only confirms things to us, but that He also corrects those things that are out of order in our lives. To be a disciple is to be disciplined.

You Can Have Personal Face-to-Face Discipleship From Jesus

It was not because I was called to the office of the apostle that He allowed me to experience this one-on-one, special, face-to-face training with Him, though we know that the call of the apostles' ministry requires face-to-face appearances of the Lord. The Scripture records that Jesus said, "If any man" which implies anyone!

> **If any man** come to me, and hate not his father, and mother, and wife, and children, and brethren, and sisters, yea, and his own life also, he cannot be **my disciple** (Luke 14:26).

This means anybody! The Holy Spirit also highlighted another point to consider in this Scripture: Jesus stressed the words *My disciple.* The word "my" stresses His personal involvement and ownership to take it upon Himself to train and discipline you. This was so awesome to me when I saw this in Scripture. This Scripture allowed me to understand that the face-to-face visitations I had were partly happening so that Jesus could teach me things in His word that I didn't quite understand.

Sometimes, I was beamed quickly into Heaven during my sleep and was brought before Jesus just so He could teach me. I'll tell you more about this later in this book. Get ready! You are about to have the same experiences as you follow the same pattern that Jesus set forth in the Scriptures to become His personal disciple.

Two of these relationships can happen simultaneously when we obey the Lord's command to do whatsoever He tells us. To be His disciple, you have to obey the command to forsake all that you have and love Him more than anyone. After the first couple of years of my salvation, the Lord called me to preach and minister His gospel while in college. This began with the servanthood level.

MY TRIP TO HEAVEN

In the very first visitation I had from Jesus, I noticed He told me to come to Him, to surrender my life to follow Him, and to leave my best friend.

This is how you can tell what level your relationship is at with the Lord when He starts coming to you face-to-face. Is he asking you to love Him more than everything else in the world and to forsake all to be obedient to Him? Is the appearance from Jesus teaching you about something that is pertaining to His personal discipleship? This is the Lord's discipleship training. Is He commissioning you in the visitation about what work or assignment He wants you to do? This would be servanthood. Or, if you and Jesus are spending time and fellowshipping alone, then you are experiencing intimacy. These aspects of relationship will often overlap, and you may experience discipleship and servanthood simultaneously. You must know the difference between each type of appearance because it helps you to discern the level on which He's relating to you and what level you're on with Him.

Do You Love Him More Than Anybody?

I had come to know Him as a teenager, but He was requiring me to love Him more than my best friend and to forsake that relationship so that I could follow Him wholeheartedly as His disciple. Then in college, He asked to me to follow Him on another level, and He moved me into the servanthood dimension. Do you know how many people, both young and old, can't do what the Lord really wants them to do because they are in godly relationships with ungodly soul ties with their wives, husbands, fathers, mothers, children, friends, and even themselves. God has given them these relationships, but they are too close and too tied to them so that when God wants them to forsake them to do His will and follow Him, it's a struggle for them. Jesus was saying to us that our love for all these relationships should look like hate compared to our love for Him. He wasn't telling us to hate the people in our lives but to love them less than Him. The word hate in this context means to love less. No one should take the place reserved in our hearts and minds for the Lord. He prizes this intimacy in your heart toward Him and you should too.

Jesus Mentions Different Dimensions of Relationship in Scripture

The disciples were first relating to Jesus as students who received personal training from Jesus. Jesus sent them out to preach the Kingdom of God and they entered another dimension of relationship called servanthood. Then we see Jesus promote His servants to friends (see John 15). The disciples transitioned through different levels of relationship all within a three-and-a-half year period while walking closely with Jesus every day. The same is with us in our walk with God.

We move from being a student and disciple of Jesus in a classroom-type atmosphere to working for the Lord by serving Him on the field. You must move from being a disciple and servant to being a friend in the same way that Jesus promoted the disciples in John 15:15. We don't get there just because He mentions this in Scripture; there are conditions to growing in our relationship with Him. The disciples paid the ultimate price by forsaking all and following Him.

> *Henceforth I call you not servants; for the servant knoweth not what his lord doeth: but I have called you friends; for all things that I have heard of my Father I have made known unto you* (John 15:15).

Jesus uses the word henceforth to tell us that from this point on He is moving us from service to friendship. This is the process that

Jesus takes us through: from discipleship training, to servanthood, and then finally to friendship. All these things were happening with me at a young age, but I lacked the word of God in my life to recognize this process or to articulate it. Now please don't misunderstand me. He doesn't stop discipling you just because you move into a friendship realm with Him. He continues to relate to you as a servant and a disciple after you have moved into friendship with God because He's continually building on these foundations of relationship in your life.

Each level of relationship that He relates to you on just increases and goes to a greater dimension. Over time you become a greater disciple, a greater servant, and a greater friend! The process never stops or dies. There will always be things He will have to teach us! Even after this process of moving into friendship with God, I was still far from being ready for my real, God-given destiny and assignment.

Level 1: The Discipleship Relationship with Jesus

Be My disciple (Luke 14:26).

If any man come to me and hate not his father and mother and wife, and children and brethren and sisters, yea and his own life also **he cannot be My disciple** (Luke 14:26).

Jesus' Conditions of Discipleship:

- Must continue in His Word (see John 8:31).

- Must deny yourself, take up your cross daily (see Luke 9:23; 14:26-27).

- Must bear fruit (see John 15:8).

- Must forsake all that you have (see Luke 14:33).

- Must love your closest relationships less than the Lord, including your own life (see Luke 14:26).

- Must come after Jesus (see Luke 9:23).

- Must not be ashamed of Him or deny Him (see Matt. 10:33; Mark 8:38; Luke 9:26).

Rewards for Being Jesus' Disciple

- Shall receive a hundredfold in relationships, land, and everything given up along with some persecution (see Matt. 19:29; Mark 10:28-31).

- Shall sit on thrones in the new world judging and governing designated nations by the Lord (see Matt. 19:27-30).

- You shall receive eternal life in the world to come (see Matt. 19:29).

- Will be appointed a kingdom by Jesus (see Luke 22:28-29).

- Will have the opportunity to eat and drink with Jesus at His personal table in His Kingdom (see Luke 22:28-30).

Level 2: The Servanthood Relationship With Jesus

My servants (John 12:26).

If any man serve Me, *let him follow me and where I am, there shall also My servant be; if any man serve me, him will My Father honor* (John 12:26).

The Conditions of Servanthood:

- Must follow Jesus (see John 12:26).

- Must be where Jesus is spiritually, physically, mentally, and emotionally (see John 12:26).

- Must be found faithful over a little (see Matt. 25:21, 23; Luke 16:10; 19:17; 1 Cor. 4:2).

- Must be wise (see Matt. 24:45).

- Must be good (see Matt. 25:23).

- Must know the Lord's will (see Luke 12:47).

- Must prepare yourself (see Luke 12:47).

Reward for Being Jesus' Servant

The Father will honour this man (John 12:26).

**Disadvantages of Being
the Lord's Servant Versus Being His Friend**

"He knoweth not what his Lord doeth" (John 15:15). He's left in the dark about what his Lord is doing unlike one who is a friend.

Level 3: Friendship With Jesus

My friends

*Ye are **My friends** if you do whatsoever I command you, **henceforth I call you not servants*** (John 15:14-15).

Conditions of Friendship With Jesus:

- We must do whatever the Lord commands us to do (see

John 15:14).

Reward for Being Jesus' Friend

- Jesus makes all things known to us that He has heard from His Father. He shares the intimate things. This is what a servant doesn't have (see John 15:15).

Level 4: Sonship With the Lord

Becoming a Son of God

> But *as many as received him*, to them gave he power to *become the sons of God*, even to them that *believe on his name* (John 1:12).

The Conditions of Sonship:

- Must believe on Jesus (see John 1:12).

- Must receive Jesus (see John 1:12).

- Must endure chastening, discipline, scourging, and rebukes from the Lord (see Heb. 12:7).

- Must be led by the Spirit of God (see Rom. 8:14).

- Must be tutored and trained in God's Word (see Gal. 4:1-2).

- Must learn obedience through suffering (see Heb. 11:8).

Reward for Being a Son

- Inheritance from God—Heirs of God (see Rom. 8:17).

- Being a joint-heir to Jesus (Jesus will become your brother). You will inherit the same things Jesus has already inherited in God's Kingdom (see Rom. 8:17).

- Will be glorified together with Jesus (see Rom. 8:17).

Note: You can review this covenant in the first book.

Level 5: The Marriage Covenant With God

**The Marriage Covenant—
God's Covenant with His "Elect"**

> *And **I will betroth thee unto me for ever**; yea, I will betroth thee unto me in righteousness, and in judgment, and in loving kindness, and in mercies; I will even betroth thee unto me in faithfulness: and thou shalt know the Lord* (Hosea 2:19-20).

Conditions of Marriage Covenant:

- Must be joined to the Lord. Becoming one in spirit and marriage with Him (see 1 Cor. 6:17)

- Must commit your body to Him in a special way, through abstaining from sin, pollution, fornication etc. Must consecrate your body wholly to the Lord forever! (See 1 Cor. 6:13-20.)

- Must prepare and make yourself ready by cleaning and purifying one's spiritual garments (see Rev. 19:7-8).

- Must have on your spiritual wedding garments with the Lord (see Matt. 22:1-14).

- Must commit and surrender to the Lord in this covenant of marriage in five ways for all eternity:

1. In righteousness

2. In Judgment

3. In loving kindness

4. In mercies

5. In faithfulness

Rewards for Being Married to the Lord—Being His Elect!

A. As you mature in your relationship with the Lord and embrace Him in a marriage covenant, He will take extra measures to protect your relationship with Him and to ensure your salvation.

B. Shortening of the end-time days to ensure the elect's salvation during chastening and perilous times (see Matt. 24:22).

C. Judging by death to ensure your salvation (see 1 Cor. 5:5; 1 Cor. 12:30-32).

D. By allowing you to be delivered over to Satan for any different form of judgment is to save you for all of eternity with immortality (see 1 Cor. 5:5).

E. He governs time, seasons, and days to ensure the immortality of His elect because He has made this marriage covenant an everlasting covenant for all of eternity with you (see Hos. 2:19; Matt. 24:22).

Note: You can review this covenant in my first book, *Face-to-Face Appearances From Jesus.*

Level 6: The Love Covenant Relationship With the Lord

Beyond the love for a spouse...

> *Very pleasant hast thou been unto me: thy love to me was wonderful, passing the love of women* (2 Samuel 1:26).

Conditions of the Love Covenant:

- Must love Him greater than the love that two married people naturally have for each other. You must even love the Lord beyond your love for Him in a marriage covenant (see 2 Sam. 1:26).

- Must love Him just as much and more than you love your own soul (see 1 Sam. 25:26; Luke 14:26).

Rewards for This Love Covenant Relationship With Jesus

- A special everlasting covenant of kindness or mercy with you and your household (anyone in your family) even after you have died and have gone to Heaven (see 2 Sam. 9:1; Isa. 55:3).

Note: You can review this covenant in my first book, *Face-to-Face Appearances From Jesus.*

Level 7: Covenant of the Right Hand Relationship With the Lord

Be Seated at God's Right Hand

> *If ye then be risen with Christ, seek those things which are above, where Christ sitteth on the right hand of God* (Colossians 3:2).

But to sit on my right hand, and on my left, is not mine to give, but it shall be given to them for whom it is prepared of my Father (Matthew 20:23).

Conditions of the Right Hand Relationship With the Lord:

- Must understand that only the Father has the authority to sit you at His own right hand next to Jesus; it is the Father's call on this (see Matt. 20:23).

- Must be prepared by the Father for this place in Jesus' life (see Matt. 20:23).

- Must never deviate from the first and greatest commandment—to love the Lord (see Matt. 22:37-38).

- Must never leave the first love you have with the Lord. Your love must increase for Him and not decrease or be lost! (See Rev. 2:1-3.)

- Must be willing to love the Lord even if it leads to your death as a martyr for Him or your fellow brother or sister on earth (see Matt. 10:38).

- Must stay on the path of ever increasing love for the Lord while living on earth (see Eph. 3:19).

- Must love Jesus beyond everything and everyone in this world (see Matt. 10:37).

- Must make loving Him the focus of your life even if it costs you everything! (See Phil. 3:7-8.)

- Must be prepared, approved, honored, and commended by the Father in your love for Jesus (see Matt. 20:23)

Reward for the Right-Hand Covenant

- The Lord Himself will be your reward and personal prize won! (See Phil. 3:8,14.)

- You will win a special relationship and close intimacy with Jesus for all eternity that very few seek or will obtain! (See Phil. 3:14; 1 Cor. 9:24-25.)

- You will be seated next to Jesus, who sits at God's right hand, by the Father Himself! (See Matt. 20:23.)

- You will be honored by God the Father on the highest level for loving His Son (see John 16:27)

- You will be honored with great authority and power in the Father's whole empire like Jesus, as well as being given a place of highest power within Jesus' own kingdom that the Father has given unto Him, within His whole empire! (See Luke 22:29-30.)

Note: You can review this covenant in my first book, *Face-to-Face Appearances From Jesus.*

Level 8: Our Covenant Relationship With Jehovah God the Father

Jesus introduces and reveals the Father to us:

> *All things are delivered unto me of my Father: and no man knoweth the Son, but the Father; neither knoweth any man the Father, save the Son, and he to whomsoever the Son will reveal him* (Matthew 11:27).

Conditions of this relationship:

- Must accept and receive Jesus first (see John 13:20; Mark 9:37; 1 John 2:23; 2 John 1:9).

- Must Love His Son Jesus first (see John 14:21,23; John 16:27).

- Must honor Jesus, God's Son (see John 5:23; 14:21, 23; 16:27).

- Must be brought to the Father and introduced to Him by Jesus (see Matt 11:27; John 14:6).

Rewards of this covenant relationship:

- The Father promises to manifest His love to us in a special way (see John 14:21,23).

- The Father Himself promises to come to us (see John 14:23).

- The Father Himself, like Jesus, will make His abode, habitation and living arrangements with us (see John 14:23).

- Jesus promised that our relationship with the Father would be promoted when He said that we would be able to go directly in prayer to the Father in Jesus' name (see John 16:26-27).

- The Father will be revealed to you by Jesus (see Matt. 11:27).

- Will get to be introduced by Jesus to meet the Father face to face—the reconciliation with God in completeness (see John 14:6; 2 Cor. 5:18-20).

Note: You can review this covenant in my first book, *Face-to-Face Appearances From Jesus.*

The Face-to-Face Teacher

The Importance and Purpose of Jesus Training Us by Appearing Face to Face

The main purpose of this chapter is to relay to you this awesome opportunity to be supernaturally trained and guided through face-to-face encounters with Jesus Christ. In contrast, many are only ever discipled by people and never experience God's personal discipleship. I am not degrading the discipleship done by God's servants through the five-fold ministry, or by any one of His believers. Jesus Himself told us to go into all the world and to make disciples (students and pupils) of all men by being their personal teacher and training them to observe everything He has taught us.

To be trained and discipled by spiritual fathers, mentors, and people of great stature and wisdom is a wonderful thing and in alignment with Scripture. This type of discipleship gives us invaluable lessons that we could not otherwise learn and saves us many years of first-hand experience. The Bible also mentions that John the Baptist had his own disciples. Elijah also modeled this when he discipled Elisha along with others called the sons of the prophets; they were students and learners under his prophetic ministry. The Bible is clear about the Lord entrusting His people to earthly teachers. But the wonderful opportunity and revelation that I'm sharing with you is that Jesus promised in Scripture to take you up as His own personal student.

He Will Be Your Face-to-Face Rabonni—Teacher

Ye call me Master [Teacher] *and Lord: and ye say well; for so I am* (John 13:13).

This title of Master, Rabonni, or Teacher concerning Jesus will become pronounced in your life just as the other manifestations of His names has such as Savior, Redeemer, or Healer have been. How would you like that? It is an awesome experience and opportunity for Jesus to not only appear to you because He loves you, but also to appear to you in dreams, open visions, trances, and out-of-body experiences like He did to the men of old in the Bible. He's doing the same today to teach and train you through these avenues. As I've spoken to you, I've shown you how Jesus has done this in my own personal life. I have seen that He has not only trained me as His personal student, but that He has also done this with my staff and those we minister to.

I teach people that they are indeed sitting under my teaching for training and discipleship, but that they can also be personally discipled by Jesus in a face-to-face way if they will count the cost and pay the price. I share that He wants to be a face-to-face teacher just like he is be a face-to-face friend. One thing that I have taught them is that, "Yes, Jesus has sent you here to sit under the teaching He has given me over the years, to train you and disciple you, but I will also introduce you to the process and the price of how to become Jesus' own face-to-face personal student like I have become. He will be a face-to-face Teacher just as I've shown you in my first book how He's been a face-to-face Friend. He has personally discipled me, and I know that He wants to personally disciple you in a similar way. This is another way that He will *manifest* Himself to you as a teacher and you will be affectionately known by Jesus as "My disciple" (see John 14:21). Isn't this awesome!

Jesus Is a Revelator of the Scriptures

Then opened he their understanding, that they might understand the Scriptures (Luke 24:45).

The Lord has entrusted my ministry with so many different precious people that He is appearing to. He is training and discipling them through face-to-face visitations concerning who He is and about the content of His Word. This type of revelatory relationship with Jesus illuminates the "gray areas" of the Bible. There are many things in the Bible that are not clearly understood, often because there are not enough details for us to clearly understand the context. For example, Jesus took me to the grave of Judas to help me understand two Scriptures surrounding Judas' death that weren't clear to me because there were missing details. The lack of details could lead anyone to be unclear about the way that his death took place.

Consider this: the Bible says in Acts that after Jesus' resurrection from the dead He appeared to His disciples and stayed with them on earth for forty days training them concerning the things pertaining to the Kingdom of God. Jesus commands us in the Scriptures to seek first the Kingdom of God. Based upon these two things, I have wanted to know the specific things Jesus trained His disciples about concerning the Kingdom for those forty days. The Scripture does not give details about the lessons taught during these forty days.

The truths that Jesus gave these men concerning the Kingdom of God had to be different and more extensive than the parables He taught them over the previous three-year period. These truths had to be on another level and in another dimension than the teachings He had previously given them concerning the Kingdom than in the earlier stages in their walk with Him. This is seen by His statement when He told them after they had faithfully served and walked with Him as His disciples and servants saying, *"I will no longer speak to you in proverbs but I will show you plainly"* (see John 16:25). Jesus said these words to His disciples, His friends, before His death on the cross. This reveals that what He taught them during those forty days about the Kingdom of God was on a different level, was with a greater intensity, and revealed new facts that would empower the disciples to turn the world upside down. I believe this forty-day training course was the icing on the cake of their three-and-one-half year course in the Kingdom of God.

I wanted to find out what these forty days of teaching covered because it has been lost in our generation! I also believe that there are a lot of things that Jesus taught the apostles that were lost and never passed on to the next generations because of the dark ages and other different factors that have taken place in history. To be effective in our generation and to recover this valuable information, we need Jesus to appear to us face to face, just like He did to the apostles after His resurrection, and we need Him to train us by bringing restoration to this valuable information about the Kingdom of God. In conclusion, no man can train us like Jesus can, so to have both is an extraordinary honor!

Being Disciplined and Trained Through Face-to-Face Encounters: Jesus Appears to Me About Slothfulness

During the first year I was away from home at college, the Lord visited me again. This was in 1990 and I was very young in the Lord then. I would call this experience face-to-face discipleship with the Lord because I was still a student and He started appearing to me to train me. I had become His personal disciple and been willing to love Him and forsake the world and all my unfruitful relationships. I was in Charleston, South Carolina, studying to be a chef, and I had only been a Christian for two years. At this time I was still learning a lot, although I didn't understand everything that was going on in my life at the time. One day a wonderful, dear saint who attended my church, Darlene, invited me to go and visit a family in our church who had lost a loved one. When we first arrived at their home, I heard the Lord tell me, *"Go to the bathroom for a few minutes and pray."* I didn't obey. If I had done what He told me to do, the following story would not have happened.

So, I didn't do what the Lord told me to do. When we went into the house and sat down, there was a spirit of sadness due to the death of their loved one. I'd like you to understand that the church that I was from taught a message of jubilee and rejoicing even in the saddest times of your life. I misinterpreted this and was very unbalanced. When I saw all the sadness, I stood up and started prophesying openly to the family in the living room telling them that God wanted them to praise Him. I stood up and told them that they needed to get up and praise Him and I meant it as a slight rebuke. I didn't understand or think about the Scriptures that tell us we are to comfort those that mourn. I wasn't comforting them in a time of bereavement—I was rebuking them. Darlene was quiet on the way home. I didn't realize that I did anything wrong, let alone an unthinkable thing.

As a young teenager, Darlene's family, the Browns, had taken care of me. They are a beautiful family and are still so special in my heart today! I'll never forget the blessing of being taken care of by them while I was away from home. When we arrived to our destination, Darlene said to me, *"David, there's something the Lord put on my heart to share with you."* She then said to me, *"Today, when you ministered to that family and prophesied to them you were off."* She went on to say, *"That was not the Lord speaking through you."* In those days God was using me, but I also made mistakes. Because God was using me a little, I was a little hotheaded and stubborn in standing on what I felt the Lord was telling me.

I responded to her by saying that I didn't receive her correction nor did I feel what she was saying to me was inspired by God. There was no small discussion on this matter. It got very heated between us when I said to her, *"I tell you what, I'll go to the Lord tonight in prayer and ask Him if you are right. If He shows me that you are right, I'll come back and apologize to you, but if He doesn't I'm going to stand on what I think to be the Lord."* Oh, I was as wrong as two left shoes, but I didn't realize it. With this, she said okay, and we parted our ways. So that very night I went to the Lord and asked Him if I was right or wrong when I prophesied to the precious family who had lost their loved one.

Jesus Rebukes and Corrects Me

When I fell asleep that night Jesus appeared to me in a dream to answer me. The dream scene started with me standing next to Jesus. As I remember, He was standing on my right-hand side. Standing in front of both of us was a vision of me. I couldn't believe it! The strange thing is that as I looked at myself, I noticed I had on mismatched shoes. One shoe was one color and the other was another. I looked all wrong. Jesus spoke for the first time in this visitation and said with a yell, *"Half-cocked!"* Then I woke up. I had heard this word being used by my dad and those of older generations, but I didn't quite know what it meant. So I called my father to ask and he told me that it means that you are partially right about a thing, but you lack the knowledge of knowing how to carry it out in the right way, which still makes you wrong. I knew what this word from God meant. I knew the Lord was confirming that He had spoken through Darlene the previous day. After this I felt so bad, broken, and convicted and went to her to tell her she was right and that I was sorry. I also thanked her for having the boldness to tell me I was wrong!

I Responded the Wrong Way to His Correction
by Becoming Slothful

But instead of being encouraged by this correction, I got discouraged. I never wanted to prophesy incorrectly again by saying that the Lord was speaking something when He wasn't. I responded incorrectly and allowed this correction to turn me toward discouragement. I picked up the wrong attitude through this correction and did not want to prophesy anymore for a long time. I even said that night that I was going to slow down in preaching God's word and in prophesying because of this mess-up. Oh, but why did I say this? I didn't know it, but this was a grave and incorrect attitude that I expressed.

I didn't respond like this without cause. You see, I was a young Christian who was very zealous for the Lord. I responded like this out of a build-up of disappointments from missing the Lord multiple times. At this time of my life, I was striving very hard to learn and know the voice of God. Let me explain. During the first two years of my walk with the Lord, I tried to learn His voice so much that I experienced many trials and errors. For example, one day I was praying and I heard what I thought was the voice of the Lord saying, *"I want you to go to the mall, and when you get there a man will be leaning against the pillar. I want you to witness to Him about Me."* There was a mall up the street from my dorm, and as a new Christian I was zealous to do good works and to do whatever I thought the Lord was saying to me. I was only 18 and had just gotten saved a little over a year earlier. So I jumped up and headed down to the mall in the rain!

Yes, it was raining, but I didn't care! All I wanted to do was obey my King Jesus, to do what I thought He was telling me! When I arrived at the mall about 10 to 20 minutes later, I went up to the pillar where I thought the Lord had directed me. To my amazement, the mall was closed and no one was there. I didn't let that discourage me. I waited in the rain thinking maybe the Lord meant this man was going to come up to the mall. Well, nothing ever happened. So I chalked it up and said, "I missed God." It was me and my own zealousness in wanting to do something for God! You can see that before I missed hearing God with Darlene, there was already a build-up of disappointment in my life from this type of scenario where I thought that the Lord had said things to me but realized later that He hadn't. I endured many let downs with joy, but the buildup of these disappointments brought me to a point of breaking.

So that's why I said, "I'm just going to slow down in witnessing or prophesying," because even though I was hearing the Lord accurately many times, I was also missing Him through trial and error. I was tired of missing it, so that's why I responded this way! How many of us act like this when we are corrected by the Lord! This stems from our fallen nature. This is one of the ways our flesh reacts to correction. That night I went back to sleep and I had another encounter with Jesus that would change the rest of my life!

Jesus Warns Me About Hell

I was visited by Jesus in a dream again. In this visitation He showed me the fires in hell. This fire didn't totally look like the fire on earth, but it had an eternal element to it. It looked strange, like no other fire I had ever seen. Then the Lord said to me, *"There are many people and preachers down here because they did not answer my call."* Then He said to me, *"If you do not preach My gospel you too will end up here..."* Then He showed me another truth that same night as I watched the vision play out on what looked like a movie screen.

Slothfulness Keeps Many From Entering
the "Straight Gate"

Jesus used different scenes in this dream to speak to me in parables. In the first scene, Jesus showed me a group of saints that were all standing in rows and I was among them. Everyone else was shining brightly, but when I looked at myself I had a dull and dim look on my face. Then words appeared as if someone wrote a note saying, *"Don't be dull; let your righteousness shine forth."* I didn't totally understand what the Lord meant. He showed me what would happen in my future and at the end of my life if I continued to slow down preaching and prophesying. It all played out before me.

Again, I saw myself waiting with a woman in a wheelchair. I was standing behind her and assisting her. We were waiting for the doctor to come as we stood outside his building. It was like he hadn't arrived there yet. To my surprise, I didn't know the doctor was going to be Jesus. He finally came toward us in His beautiful, white robe, but He walked past us like He didn't know us. In this scene, I knew that He knew us, but He just walked past us like He didn't know us.

Then He went into this beautiful glass building that was His place, and the door shut behind Him. I pursued Him when I saw that He didn't acknowledge us standing there. As I got to the door that shut behind Him, I started knocking and tried to get in saying, "Let me in," but He would never come to the door. Then I remembered saying these last words, "If I could just get in." With this, the scene on the picture screen ended and there was a still hush and quietness. Then without seeing Jesus anymore, I was back in my body.

I was in a deep sleep, but conscious that I was sleeping too deeply to wake up on my own when I heard a gentle, peaceful voice that shook me to the core of my being, and is still shaking me now. Jesus said to me, *"Strive to enter in at the straight gate, for many shall seek to enter in but shall not be able because of slothfulness."* Then His voice paused for a moment until he concluded by saying, *"The first shall be last and the last shall be first."* This voice was so powerful but soft. It had such a gentle, still, serene sound of quietness and peace in it that shook my entire being!

I Didn't Understand the Depth of His Love in Chastisement

With this I woke up; it was very early in the morning about 3:00 to 4:00 A.M. I saw that it was dark outside my window. I was sweating. This visitation put such a fear of God in my heart. I had only been saved for one-and-one-half years; plus it was my first year in college, and He was gently teaching me in love. He was correcting me early in my walk just like the Bible says, ***"He that loveth him chasteneth him betimes"*** (Prov. 13:24). Today, I am so thankful that the Lord dealt with me in this way when I was a young man and in the early stages of my walk with Him, although I didn't always understand what was happening. From the moment I woke up, I made up my mind to never say again what I said to cause this dream! I was new in my Christian walk, and I was still learning the Bible, but I remembered reading that Jesus said something about the straight gate in the Gospels. So I got my Bible and turned to it.

*Then said one unto Him, **Lord, are there few that be saved? And he said unto them. Strive to enter in at the strait gate; for many, I say unto you, will seek to enter in, and shall not be able. When once the master of the house is risen up, and hath shut to the door. and ye begin to stand without, and to knock at the door, saying, Lord, Lord, open unto us; and He shall answer and say unto you, I know you not whence ye are:** Then shall ye begin to say, We have*

*eaten and drunk in thy presence and theou has taught in
our streets. But He shall say, I tell you, **I know you not
whence ye are**; depart from Me, all ye workers of iniquity…And, behold, **there are last which shall be first,
and there first which shall be last** (Luke 13:23-30).*

After I finished reading all of this, I was astonished. I said to
myself, "I've just seen this whole scenario that Jesus described
to me in the dream here in the Word." In the second scene of my
dream we were standing outside the door and Jesus acted as if He
didn't know us, even though I knew we were acquainted. I saw
that this dream matched His words in the Bible! In my dream I had
stood outside the door knocking and asking to come in, but He did
not acknowledge me just like the Scripture said He wouldn't.

In this same dream He also showed me that I wouldn't be saved
if I kept the attitude of discouragement I had; I later would come
to find out that this was an inward spiritual condition of slothfulness. He said to strive or I wouldn't get in because of slothfulness.
I didn't understand what slothfulness was because most Christians
look at it differently than He does!

I went back to reading the Scripture further and I found that
Jesus essentially started talking about this whole subject because
someone asked him the question, *"Lord are there few that be saved?"*
(Luke 13:23). This whole parable, teaching, and warning that Jesus
gave had to do with salvation. Here in this context Jesus was teaching another nugget concerning the *"knowledge of salvation"* mentioned in **Luke 1:17**. I learned later that the Lord was trying to warn
me and keep me out of hell through this gentle rebuke in this visitation. You see, He was saying, as it states in His word, *"…many will
seek to enter into the strait gate,"* (see Luke 13:24) (Heaven or Eternal Life in God's Kingdom) but shall not be able to enter for many
different reasons. He specifically told me that one of the things I
needed to deal with at the time was slothfulness.

The Knowledge of Salvation

You see there is knowledge of salvation. A lot of people in the church are going to go to hell and not know why. Jesus was not talking about my mistakes but my attitude. To help you understand this further, I will share another experience similar to this. It was a time when I had gotten very discouraged and disheartened, and I totally stopped praising God and praying. One night during this time, I was asleep and the Lord visited me again, but I didn't see Him. All I heard was His still, soft, quiet voice saying, *"David, you're on your way to hell."* Then I replied, *"Why Lord, I've repented of my sins and the things that I've done against You."* Then He said, *"I know; that's not the problem."* I asked Him again, "Lord, why?" Then He replied, *"Because you have stopped being My partner in praise and prayer."* Then I woke up. I wondered what being the Lord's partner in praise and prayer had to do with my salvation. I thought, *"I am saved by grace through faith, and I believe that Jesus died on the cross for me."* Later I learned that we are saved by grace through faith, not by works, nor because of our own merit, but that there are other components to our salvation that the Bible mentions that keep us in salvation and on the path to eternal life.

There is knowledge of salvation that the Bible speaks about, but we don't understand it in our day. We take one Scripture and run with it. As time went on, I also understood that the Lord was talking about my attitude and not my faults, weaknesses, and shortcomings. You see sin has been dealt with. It is the attitudes we have that will either keep us on course or cause us to be led out of the way.

> *Wherefore lift up the hands which hang down, and the feeble knees; And make straight paths for your feet, lest that which is lame be turned out of the way; but let it rather be healed* (Hebrews 12:12-13).

41

The lame areas or shortcomings and weaknesses in our lives are not the problem. The problem is that we have bad attitudes and actions that don't allow healing or mending to occur in our lives. The Bible encourages us to lift up the hands that hang down, which speaks of a form of praising or surrender to God in worship after we are chastened or corrected by the Lord.

This is how the Bible teaches us to act in these circumstances after being chastened by God. I've heard people say, "So, you are saying that our total salvation is predicated upon all these things and not in what Jesus did alone on the cross when He purchased our salvation with His blood?" No, I'm not saying that. I would never belittle the work that only Jesus Himself could do to bring us back into right fellowship with God. Jesus purchased our salvation, but the point I'm trying to make is that once you are saved, you can lose your salvation in many different ways. There is no such thing as once saved, always saved! If this is true then you would have to take out the Scripture in Revelation that our names can be blotted out of the book of life (see Rev. 3:5). If it is not possible for one to lose their salvation then why does the Scripture state this?

The Lord has given us different components to salvation that will keep us on the path of eternal life, and two of them are praise and rejoicing. The best way I can explain this is to use an analogy my good friend Jim Wilcox shared with me. Jim is a pilot and the words he shared were shocking and revelatory and helped explain what the Lord had been trying to teach me. He told me that when a pilot is flying an airplane from St. Louis to Chicago, he can fly 2 degrees off course, and he will still arrive at his destination in Chicago. But if he is off the same 2 degrees when flying from St. Louis to Los Angeles those 2 degrees add up due to the long distance, and by the time he reaches his destination he would be in another city. You can be just 2 degrees off and end up in left field somewhere far away from your original target.

It's the same here with salvation. While we are on our way to enter eternal life through the straight gate we must stay on course to arrive at the gate of Heaven. The Lord has given us certain wisdom and knowledge of how to stay on the path of life to salvation. He puts us on the path of salvation by His purchase on Calvary, but we must stay on that path.

I Was Working Out My Salvation

When I woke up I pondered how this could be. I could understand Jesus telling me I was on my way to hell if He had said it when I made some of the biggest mistakes of my Christian walk. You see, sin is not the problem with Jesus, because sin is what He came to take care of and died for in our lives. Instead, the problem is the attitudes we hold when we don't respond well to failures, circumstances, and trials.

The Lord confirmed this to me several times. I turned on a Christian television network, Trinity Broadcast Network (TBN), and at that moment Joyce Myers was on and she said, *"Praise has something to do with your salvation."* Later that day I was still watching TBN and someone else said the same thing: praise has something to do with our salvation. Thank God for TBN and Christian television; I've been greatly blessed by TBN! This was confirmation to me, but I still didn't understand it until the Holy Spirit opened the Scriptures to me. Then I searched and saw it clearly when it said;

> *Therefore with joy* [praise, rejoicing] *shall ye draw waters out of the wells of salvation* (Isaiah 12:3).

We draw the waters of salvation out of the well of salvation (our belly). Jesus refers to this well in John 7:38 where he says that there is a well in us that is springing up into everlasting life. Joy serves as the bucket for us to draw the waters of salvation life.

How awesome! To confirm this, God showed me David's life after he sinned. He prayed, *"Restore unto me the joy of thy salvation"* (Ps. 51:12 ASB). Joy has a lot to do with our salvation. It is an important component to our destiny in salvation.

So by all these confirmations I started understanding what the Lord was saying about praise. Then on top of this, He gave me the Scripture in Isaiah 64:5 that says, ***"That meetest Him who rejoiceth and worketh righteousness."*** The Lord said to me from this Scripture that our praise brings Him on the scene and into our situation to help us. Without this help we are hopeless. The Bible also says the Lord inhabits the praises of His people. Praise brings God down into our situation no matter how bad the problem is. So whatever you do, don't ever stop praising God or being His praise partner.

The Lord also showed me that our prayer life is connected with our salvation. ***"...whosoever shall call upon the name of the Lord shall be saved"*** (Acts 2:21). The phrase "calling on God" speaks of prayer. It is a form of praying. Prayer is of utmost importance, but my attitude that motivates my joy, praise, and prayer is even more important. I allowed myself to be affected by the circumstances I was going through. I had stopped praising and being joyful in the God of my salvation. I had stopped communing with Him! In His love and mercy toward me, He would never let me go a long time without correcting me. That's the covenant He and I have.

There are many Christians who never experience this level of intimacy with the Lord so that when they have bad attitudes the Lord does not correct them personally. We do many things without knowing the magnitude of the effect it has on our salvation. Having this intimate relationship with the Lord keeps Him in your face at all times about everything. Even just one face-to-face encounter with the Lord can preserve your life like Jacob recounts,

> *...For I have seen God face to face and my life is preserved* (Genesis 32:30).

Jesus Is an Austere Person:
Understanding the Firm, Strict Side of Jesus

Jesus has an austere aspect of his personality. We see this demonstrated when he threw the money collectors out of the temple because they had defiled His Father's temple as they sold their merchandise. The word austere comes from the Greek word *austeros*,[2] which means *to be harsh or severe.* What many don't understand is that the Lord has a severe side.

> *Behold therefore the goodness and severity of God...* (Romans 11:22).

This means He will exercise a sternness and firmness when He has to, in certain cases, and you must understand that about Him or else you will be deceived by a perception of false love.

Many saints today are in deception about the Lord's love, thinking that He is so loving (which He is), and that He could never be firm, hard, or severe in His judgments or decisions. This is deception! If you don't have a balanced view of who the Lord is, you will be deceived by seeing just one side of His character. This is how I erred as a young Christian; I didn't understand enough sides and angles of the Lord's character to balance out my perception of Him. As Christians we must understand all the angles and sides of the Lord that are mentioned in the Bible: the height, depth, length, and breadth of Christ (see Eph. 3:18).

As a young Christian, I understood more about the austere side of the Lord than I did about His love. You see, having an unhealthy perspective of His severity can deceive you just like having an unhealthy perspective about His love. Most prophets fall into this category because the Lord develops a firm nature in them that enables them to deal with sin and bring correction to the body of Christ. They understand more of the Lord's sharp severity in His

45

dealings with His people. This severity of the Lord also includes the temporal and eternal punishments and judgments that we can experience. Jesus warned us of this when He said,

> *But I will forewarn you whom ye shall fear: Fear him,*
> *which after he hath killed hath power to cast into hell; yea,*
> *I say unto you, Fear him* (Luke 12:5).

It is important that we understand this side of Jesus so that we don't become unbalanced and deceived by His love for us or by our love and service for Him. The Lord corrects this imbalance when He says:

> *Many will say to me in that day, **Lord, Lord, have we***
> ***not prophesied in thy name? and in thy name have***
> ***cast out devils? and in thy name done many won-***
> ***derful works? And then will I profess unto them, I***
> ***never knew you: depart from me, ye that work iniq-***
> ***uity*** (Matthew 7:22-23).

These men were deceived by the good works they were doing in the Lord's name. Evidently they thought because they were able to work miracles and to prophecy in His name that they were in right standing and approved by Him, but this was not the case at all.

Comprehending Why He Will Deny Us:
He Will Disown You

Jesus responded in exactly the opposite way to them. Jesus said that He would declare He never knew them, which means that *He was never in an approving connection with them!* This seems harsh, but we must understand the Lord in His fullness. He will deny you! (See Matthew 10:33, Luke 12:9.) He will act as if He never knew you.

I was blessed to experience this painful rebuke from Jesus in a face-to-face visitation that changed my life, and it sobered me up! He acted as if He did not know me. I experienced the austere side of the Lord. Don't think that just because you have experienced His beautiful presence and have been taught by Him through great revelation of the Word that He approves of you. No! Make sure He approves of you beyond these manifestations of His presence in your life.

> *When once the master of the house is risen up, and hath shut to the door, and ye begin to stand without, and to knock at the door, saying, Lord, Lord, open unto us;* **and he shall answer and say unto you, I know you not whence ye are:** *Then shall ye begin to say,* **We have eaten and drunk in thy presence, and thou hast taught in our streets. But he shall say, I tell you, I know you not whence ye are; depart from me, all ye workers of iniquity** (Luke 13:25-27).

The deception is that you can get so overwhelmed by this great love that you also lose sight of His severity, which is a part of His love and it is just as important. This severity from the Lord is mostly applied in the areas of our lives where we have been disobedient, rebellious, or have disregarded a direct command from Him in some way. The severity of the Lord also manifests toward those whose characters are very evil while they are yet working for the Lord.

> *Many will say to me in that day, Lord, Lord, have we not prophesied in thy name? and in thy name have cast out devils? and in thy name done many wonderful works?* (Matthew 7:22)

Judging by their response, we can see that these men didn't know that they were in a disapproving connection with Lord. This

47

means that Jesus will allow people to do many wonderful works in His name without telling them that He is not in approval with their character. Jesus is meek and this is how a meek person operates: they don't volunteer information until asked. I don't ever want Jesus to say to me, "I never knew you." How hurtful that would be. I've experienced it in this dream, and it was painful and my heart started racing! Lift your hands now and ask the Lord, *"Lord, make me acceptable in your sight."*

Scripture mentions several situations that Jesus will deny or disown us in. The first He mentions is for not doing His Father's will. Doing the Father's will includes living right by our character, obeying His word in the way we treat people, and by keeping His commandments. In another place in Scripture, Jesus says He will deny us if we deny Him or are ashamed of Him. We deny Him when we use our mouths to say that we don't know Him, or when we act like we don't know Him in front of others. Jesus went so far as to tell us that He will disown us to His Father and His angels when we deny Him before men. Wow! That's harsh and severe! Some do not grasp the magnitude of this! Titus says that we can also deny Him by claiming to be Christians but living a corrupt, wicked, and grotesquely sinful life.

> *They profess that they know God; but in works they deny him, being abominable, and disobedient, and unto every good work reprobate* (Titus 1:16).

Jesus Hates Slothfulness

The "Slothfulness" Visitation

In this visitation the Lord was trying to show me that my own personal problem at the time was slothfulness. Jesus tells us to, *"Strive to enter in at the straight gate."* (See Luke 13:24.) He doesn't tell us to seek to enter the straight gate. Those who seek will not be able to get in; only those who strive to enter will be admitted. There is a difference in seeking and striving. The word strive comes from the Greek word *agonizomai*[3] which is the root word for *agony*. *Agonizomai* means *to struggle as to compete for a prize*, or *to contend with an adversary* (your flesh, the world, and the devil). It also means *to endeavor to accomplish something through fighting or laboring fervently*. I know that there are people out there who would say that I'm proposing a works doctrine, but I am really proclaiming that we are saved by grace through faith and not by works.

The type of works that this Scripture is talking about has nothing to do with the work or effort we are instructed to do to enter into eternal life. We must labor to enter into this rest. We must fight the good fight of faith by striving or laboring to keep our faith so that we can say, like Paul, that we have fought the good fight and kept our faith. We must strive since faith is a component to salvation. Even Jesus prayed that Peter's faith wouldn't fail (see Luke 22:32). We are saved by grace through faith. Our faith is what the enemy fights for, because it is our victory that overcomes the world. Jesus said that the work of God is to believe on Him in whom the Father has sent (see John 6:29).

The Scripture also says to work out your own salvation with fear and trembling! (See Philippians 2:12.) So striving is an important component in our salvation if we are going to keep it. There are those who think that believers have no responsibility in their salvation because Jesus paid the ultimate price for it. Yes, Jesus freely gave us salvation; that is correct. However, the Bible also teaches that we must do something to keep and steward the salvation that Jesus gave us. Just because Jesus gave us our salvation freely does not mean that he also stewards it for us too. We must also do our part to maintain such a precious, free gift. We mishandle and cheapen the grace of our Lord when we handle our salvation any other way. He paid an expensive price for our salvation. Now that we have obtained it, we must treat it preciously!

Jesus said, **"Those who seek to enter in shall not be able."** The Greek word for seek is *zeteo* and in this context means *to desire and inquire after*. It also means *to worship God.*[4] This means that it is not enough to just attend church, worship God, or simply desire to go to Heaven and be saved. These types of people do not endeavor, fight, work, or strive against the things in their life that keep them out of Heaven. They are casual seekers of God. I wanted to be saved from hell, so I started striving to enter into the straight gate.

He Disciples Us With Proverbs and Parables

These things have I spoken unto you in proverbs: but the time cometh, when I shall no more speak unto you in proverbs, but I shall show you plainly of the Father (John 16:25).

This is what Jesus was trying to get through to me, but I didn't understand it until years later. My problem was a lack of study and research in His word. In my early years I didn't search the meanings of the words in the original languages of Scripture. I didn't search the Scriptures as Jesus commanded us! Because of my lack of study, I couldn't get the full revelation of my dream. Because dreams deal with so much symbolism and are filled with many parables and metaphors from God, it is difficult to understand what He is saying if you don't search the Bible for answers. Then years later, I received the most glorious revelation and understanding through another visitation.

Jesus Teaches Me About Slothfulness

I didn't understand the Lord's definition of slothfulness. I grew up thinking slothfulness was laziness or not wanting to work. I didn't understand what slothfulness had to do with my desire to slow down in preaching and prophetic ministry because of my mistake with Darlene's friends and the lack of accuracy in what I heard from God. I was also discouraged, and I had the attitude to back off. I didn't realize this at the time, but my attitude was what prompted the Lord to respond to me in correction. I kept asking God, "What did I do?"

I also thought to myself, *I've been working by witnessing in the streets for hours this last year and one-half of my salvation. How am I slothful?* I still thought that slothfulness had to do with being lazy. You see, I was scared because Jesus had provoked the fear of the Lord in me. I wanted to find out what I had really done wrong so that I could make it into Heaven and not go to hell. As I have matured in the Lord over the years, I began to see obedience to God as an opportunity to be close with the Lord in Heaven for all Eternity and not just a way to escape Hell!

I wondered what Jesus meant when He said to me, *"Because of slothfulness."* He doesn't give a specific reason in Scripture. He just said, **"They shall not be able"** (see Luke 13:24). He never gave a reason like slothfulness in the Scripture, so it dawned on me that He was personally dealing with me!

I read a book by Rick Renner called *Sparkling Gems from the Greek*[5] years after I had the dream in which God told me that I was going to Hell because of slothfulness. I realize now that I could have learned this lesson much earlier, but I didn't know how to study God's Word the right way. I'm not saying that I didn't study at all, because I meditated on God's Word day and night when I was a young Christian. I knew Scriptures and what they said, but I didn't understand what they meant through inductive research.

It's not enough to mediate on God's Word day and night; Jesus also told us to search the Scriptures.

The Definition of True Slothfulness

In his book, Renner shares that God spoke to him about slothfulness. Renner had also associated slothfulness with laziness. He also wondered why the Lord would refer to him as being lazy when he had been very busy doing the work of the Lord. The Lord replied to him, *"I didn't say a word to you about laziness; you are a good worker, and I would not accuse you of laziness. You are slothful, and I want you to eradicate this slothfulness from your life."* As a result of this, he recognized that there is a difference between laziness and slothfulness.

Renner researched and discovered that slothfulness comes from the Greek word *nothros,* which means something that is dull. Wow; stop there! That's what the Lord was showing me in the first part of the dream; I saw myself as dull, but everyone else was shining. Then I saw the sign that said: "Don't be dull, let your righteousness shine forth."

I played the vision out again and saw that in the first scene of the dream, Jesus showed me hell. Then Jesus spoke to me about slothfulness. Until I read Renner's book, I didn't understand how the first scene related to the second scene. But this is not all!

Nothros could be compared to a candle that no longer burns brightly as it once did. Its flame has dwindled to more of a flicker than of its original intensity. The candle still gives light, but not the way it did before. The word *nothros* doesn't present the picture of laziness; rather, it speaks of **someone who has lost his zeal or his intense conviction about a matter that once was of great importance to them**. It denotes a person who has become disinterested and whose zeal has been replaced with a middle-of-the-road, take-it-or-leave-it mentality.

Renner explains that *nothros* means "monontous or unexciting." It refers to something that is slow and sluggish, or better yet something that has lost its speed or momentum. This something is still moving, but it isn't moving with the same aggressiveness it once had. It has lost the drive, thrust, pace, and speed it once possessed. This word presents here the analogy of someone who was once zealous about something, but whose zeal has now dissipated. It has been replaced instead by neutrality."

I thank God for men in the Body of Christ who write books with revelation from God in them.

The Lord will often use anointed books to reinforce what He's said to you or to enlighten you on a topic.

Stay on Fire and Don't Lose Your Zeal

Slothfulness has nothing to do with the amount of energy you or I put out to do a job. Instead it speaks of an inward condition. Even though it may externally look like we're laboring hard and going somewhere, inwardly we're stuck in neutral and going nowhere. After reading Rick Renner's book, I realized that the Lord was correcting me on my attitude of slothfulness. Remember, I had said to myself after Darlene corrected me, "I'm going to slow down in preaching and prophesying God's word." That was a slothful attitude that would have caused me to lose my speed, momentum, and velocity in the spirit that I had attained at the time with God. I didn't see how dangerous this attitude of discouragement was at the time.

Don't Cool Off Toward the Lord When You Are Rebuked by Him

I now saw that my attitude wasn't just one of discouragement, but that it had developed into a nonchalant attitude with a drawback spirit. I also saw how I was cooling off toward the Lord because of His correction to me. Instead of being zealous and repentant like Jesus told us to be when we are rebuked by Him, I did the opposite (see Rev. 3:1). I didn't get brighter; I got duller! The word *zealous* in the Greek means "To have warmth for."[6] It gives the picture of someone affectionately warming up toward you versus cooling off, which is what I was doing when I got corrected by the Lord in the first dream. Maybe you have observed this in someone you corrected or disagreed with. Instead of warming up to you, they cool down, or turn completely against you. You can observe the fruit of slothfulness when the Lord corrects a person about something and he or she begins to respond the way I did! This was a grave mistake, but many of us have been this way. I realized that this was what real slothfulness is like. It is an attitude resulting from an inward condition. Slothfulness is a heart thing.

How free I became. This truth made me free! So, anytime we cool off toward the Lord, we have lost our zeal or warmth with excitement for the things of God. This causes us, in turn, to slow down and to lose speed and momentum in our walk with God. This attitude of slothfulness is a sin. We must repent and get on course after we realize we are slothful. Thank You Jesus!

Many, Jesus said, will not enter the straight gate because of slothfulness. I now see why! If you are slothful with this type of attitude, you are not going to strive to enter; instead you will casually pursue getting in! Slothfulness can cause you to miss eternal life! If you are serious about serving and pleasing God, you must view any loss of your passion, momentum, and desire for the Lord or His service as totally unacceptable! You can get back on track again by deciding to turn from slothfulness and neutrality. You can remove this hindrance from your life! It was through this dream and Rick Renner's book that I saw that I struggled with this sin in my life. I saw that I have more of a tendency to act this way when the Lord corrects me, or when I became discouraged in serving Him.

Warm Up Toward Him Instead

The times Jesus appeared to me were to show me glimpses of His ministry when He walked this earth. I saw Him as He was, always moving with speed, purpose, and being focused on what His Father wanted Him to do. He was always moving aggressively toward the next thing that He was assigned to do. I saw the many times that I started and stopped, went forward then regressed. I didn't keep up the pace with Him like I should have, and over the years I lost my momentum in Him. All of this was a result of slothfulness in my life but without revelation I didn't recognize that this is what it was! After I gained revelation on slothfulness I realized that many of us are doing things that hinder our faith, but we don't recognize it or understand how grave a mistake it is to make. We lack this knowledge because we do not study. Jesus hates slothfulness. He's busy about His Father's business. He's diligent in business, fervent, hot, and brightly shining in spirit! Remember when He said to His mother and father,

> *...How is it that ye sought me? wist ye not that I must be about my Father's business?* (Luke 2:49)

We must keep His pace to keep up with Him. Jesus is always busy about His Father's business. He's diligent and we should be too!

His Discipleship Continues: He Trains Me Face to Face in His Miracle Healing Ministry

He Taught Me the Difference Between Miracles and Healings

In 1992, the Lord revealed to me in a dream to leave my parent's house and the familiar surroundings of Memphis, Tennessee.

I obeyed the command of the Lord and moved to Charleston, South Carolina, where he instructed me to continue fasting. I obeyed Him! In those days I would witness on the streets to the unsaved, and I also visited hospitals and prayed for the sick. I didn't have the understanding about healing that I do today, and I thought that healing was supposed to happen instantly! When I would pray for someone who was sick, some would be instantly healed, but others were not healed instantly, and I often got discouraged. After a long day of witnessing and praying for the sick on the streets in Charleston, South Carolina, I started to pray out of a place of discouragement. I was weeping, pounding on the floor, and crying out to the Lord for an answer as to why everyone I prayed for wasn't healed. You see, I thought it was supposed to happen that way for everyone.

Well, as I spoke these words to the Lord, I dropped off to sleep and immediately fell into a dream. In this dream Jesus had on a beautiful white robe and when He walked by me I repeated my question. I said to Him, *"Why isn't everyone I pray for in your name healed instantly like your Word says?"* He then looked at me with a gentle, loving look in His eyes and said, *"David, there is a difference between miracles and healings."* Then He said, *"I don't give everyone a miracle but I give some a healing!"* We spoke face-to-face while He explained to me the difference between miracles and healings. He said, *"Miracles happen instantly, but healings happen gradually."* Then He said, *"Healing is just what it means: a process of mending."*

The word *healing* is self-explanatory. When someone is healing they are in the process of being mended. After He said these words to me I woke up, and I searched the Scriptures concerning what Jesus had told me about miracles and healings. I studied His ministry on the earth and to my amazement I learned that He didn't give everyone a miracle nor did He instantly heal all who came to Him. The Bible says that some were healed in the same hour! This means they were not healed immediately like other accounts that the Bible mentions. This was an awesome discovery to me! It meant so much to me that Jesus would come to me personally and teach me this face to face.

Jesus Is Active and Zealous About His Father's Business

It's important to notice the details of your dreams because they are often very important. Don't miss any detail! In this dream, I was observing Jesus and His disciples when they walked the earth. I saw Jesus preaching and healing people as He was going from place to place. I noticed two things about Jesus in this dream, and I also noticed something about my character as well. The first time He passed by me, He was moving so fast and with diligence that I made up my mind to put myself in front of Him to ask Him this question about healing. He was going about His Father's business, and He was doing this with diligence. And, I could hardly keep up with Him!

Face-to-Face Appearance of Servanthood

He Anoints Me to Be His Servant

He's Looking for People Who Will Stand on the Authority of His Word

From 1989 to 1992, about two and one-half years, the Lord took me through a season of discipleship. When I arrived in Charleston, South Carolina, the Lord met me again in my sleep to explain to me what was on His heart and what He was looking for from me in the upcoming season. I began to notice that the Lord shifted His focus in the visitations from teaching and instruction to commissioning and commanding me with mandates and divine assignments. I entered into a new level of servanthood with the Lord. Now my life and walk with Him were taking on a drastic turn as He began commissioning me to be His servant.

It was during this period that Jesus appeared to me to answer questions I had concerning the latter rain. Suddenly I was with Him in the air above a church. Jesus had on the most beautiful white robe that I had ever seen! Every time he appears to me His robe looks more glorious to me. As I stood beside Jesus, high above the church, I saw what appeared to be a huge, golden vessel in His hands that had beautiful, golden, latter-rain anointing oil in it. I knew He wanted to pour the full contents of this vessel out on His church but could not.

He said, *"David, I brought you here to answer your questions concerning why you don't see My power in the church."* Then He began pointing things out to me that were going on in His church that He wasn't pleased with. The first thing He showed me was that some of those in the pews, the youth and adults alike, were committing sexual sin and fornication; there was so much flesh in operation in His house. Secondly, He pointed out to me the choir, those who led praise and worship, and that they brought Christian rap into His house and started singing. He was so displeased by this! I saw it in the expression on His face when He pointed it out to me.

He Called Me Into Ministry and Urged Me to Be Faithful to Him

Then He instructed me to correct and rebuke those in His house. As I did this, He did something that was unusual. While dipping one of His fingers in the latter-rain, glory oil He looked at me and said, *"Be faithful."* Then He stretched out His finger over the church and allowed one drop to hit the whole church. When this drop fell from His finger it sprayed or sprinkled into drops of rain onto the people. When the drop hit the congregation, the whole crowd erupted in spontaneous praises. It was high praise and very beautiful to watch. The move of God caused by the drop died out. Jesus and I stood there, and I knew that He wanted to pour out the fullness of the latter-rain on His church but couldn't because it was short-circuited by sin, the flesh, and worldliness.

Jesus brought another problem He was displeased with to my attention. He showed me the pastor standing at His pulpit. The pastor saw all these wrong things going on in the congregation and in the choir but he wouldn't speak out against them. Jesus was very displeased with this Shepherd who allowed all these things to take place in the Lord's house. I saw the pastor of the church preaching while He was lying flat on his back. Jesus then showed me that a lot of His leaders and pastors were preaching His word, but they were doing it while lying down instead of standing up! He then instructed me to intercede for His pastors and leaders. Oh, I do intercede for them, because I love God's Shepherds so much. They go through a lot. Jesus put me back in my body, but I was still in a deep sleep when I heard a voice that said these words that shook me, *"I need a man who will stand on the authority of My word!"*

He Gave Me My First Assignment and Commissioned Me

It was the voice of Jesus. My whole being was shaking and trembling because I realized that He didn't say, *"David, I need you to stand on the authority of my word!"* Instead, He said he needed a man and He left the choice up to me. The Almighty Son of God was looking for a man to do this.

> *And I sought for a man among them, that should make up the hedge, and stand in the gap before me for the land, that I should not destroy it: but I found none* (Ezekiel 22:30).

I decided I would be this man, knowing He wouldn't have brought this to my attention if He didn't want me to respond. I was completely shaken in my whole being from His words. They went through me like liquid fire. From that experience I received my commission from the Lord: to be a man who would stand on the authority of His word. Then suddenly I woke up. I was still shaking. It was very early in the morning around 4:00 A.M.

I felt currents of electricity going through my whole being! My body was trembling with currents of liquid fire that went through me from my head down all the way to my feet. My whole heart cried out in response to Him when He shared the need and His desire for a man who would stand on the Authority of His word! I said, "Lord, I'll be faithful in doing it." At this point, the Lord revealed to me that this rebuke was going to be the prerequisite of the latter-rain glory that He wants to pour out on His Church.

Chapter 2

REMOVING THE VEILS:

Experiencing Change When Jesus Appears to You Face to Face

Open Face

Is Your Face Covered or Open?
He Wants to Be Face to Face With You

JESUS WANTS NOTHING hindering His direct face-to-face relationship with you. You must behold Him with an open face when He comes to you face to face. Just because He comes to us face to face in His Glory does not necessarily mean He is making contact with our face or the very essence of us. This is because our faces have been covered by so many veils, the residue of past and present experiences that separate us from seeing Him plainly as He really is. I wondered why I still lacked in many areas of my life even though I had experienced many face-to-face encounters with the Lord. I had read that as we behold Him and His glory we are changed:

> *But we all, with open face beholding as in a glass the glory of the Lord, are changed into the same image from glory to glory, even as by the Spirit of the Lord* (2 Corinthians 3:18).

This change wasn't happening in me completely. I knew something was wrong. I had also studied First John 3:2, which says, *"... when he shall appear, we shall be like him; for we shall see him as he is."* The Lord gave me revelation that we are changed into His likeness and image when we behold Him in the proper way. I missed two important factors in both of these Scriptures. In the first, I missed that the Bible says that we must behold Him with an open face. That means our face must not be covered by any veils, which block us from being changed when we see Him. In the second Scripture, I missed the point that we must see Him as He really is in order to be like Him. So the point is not just that we see Him. We must view Him with an open face that is free from the veils that cloud our vision and heart and distort our real view of Him.

Veils Distort Truth

Veils are mindsets, opinions, or things that distort our view of who Jesus is, preventing us from seeing things the way they really are. Veils are a form of deception. These veils keep you from seeing things and situations the way God does. Remove the veils! When veils are removed from our faces, we can then see Him as He is. When he comes, your face must be open and free from these veils. Is your face open? This is why I wasn't being changed like I know I should have been after experiencing Him in so many of these face-to-face encounters! He gave me the key to removing these veils and I'm going to share it with you!

Removing the Veils So You Can See Him Clearly Face- to Face

Beloved, we must remove these veils from our faces so we can see Him plainly when He arrives. This is where I made the mistake in my walk with Him, but I was too immature to understand.

Removing veils from our face speaks of removing every distorted, religious, worldly or fleshly opinion or view about Jesus or life itself. This also includes anything that has formed in our conscience and has become a part of our decisions or thought making process. These dysfunctional thoughts and processes stem from personal or individual circumstances, trials, pains, hurts, teachings, and false doctrines of men. These also include our failures and/or dysfunctional beliefs from our culture and the ethnical values of our race taught to us by our ancestors.

That is not God's way! The list goes on. All these things distort the view of who Jesus really is and what He is like. If you don't get rid of these veils by exposure to truth, which causes them to be removed, you can receive a face-to-face visitation from the Lord but never get the full effect of the change that's supposed to take place in your life as a result of beholding His face.

Being Changed by the Visitation From Jesus

The Bible says that these veils are places in our life where our view is distorted in some way because we lack the truth in our life.

> *But if the ministration of death, written and engraven in stones, was glorious, so that the children of Israel could not stedfastly behold the face of Moses for the glory of his countenance; which glory was to be done away: How shall not the ministration of the spirit be rather glorious? And not as Moses, which put a veil over his face, that the children of Israel could not stedfastly look to the end of that which is abolished: But their minds were blinded: for until this day remaineth the same vail untaken away in the reading of the old testament; which vail is done away in Christ. But even unto this day, when Moses is read, the vail is upon their heart* (2 Corinthians 3:7-8,13-15).

Beloved, now are we the sons of God, and it doth not yet appear what we shall be: but we know that, when he shall appear, we shall be like him; for we shall see him as he is (1 John 3:2).

The Bible also explains that God gave us our heart to understand things with, but that veils can distort things so that we do not see the way He does. When a couple gets married, the bride (which represents the Church) wears a veil over her face. Until the veil is lifted from her face, she sees her engaged spouse through the filmy, colored distortion of the veil she's looking through. We can become the same way toward Jesus. We can allow the truth of the word to remove these veils by asking Him for deeper, absolute truth in the areas of our life that are distorted. The Bible says He will take them away so that we can behold Him with an open face and be changed into His image. Jesus prayed to the Father that we would share in the glory and image that He and the Father have had since the beginning of the world (see John 17:24). He wants us to experience that same glory He experienced with the Father. Wow, this is awesome! The Lord takes these veils away from us by the process He calls judgment.

The fear of the Lord is clean, enduring for ever: the judgments of the Lord are true and righteous altogether. More to be desired are they than gold, yea, than much fine gold: sweeter also than honey and the honeycomb. Moreover by them is thy servant warned: and in keeping of them there is great reward. Who can understand his errors? cleanse thou me from secret faults. Keep back thy servant also from presumptuous sins; let them not have dominion over me: then shall I be upright, and I shall be innocent from the great transgression (Psalm 19:9-13).

These judgments of the Lord help cleanse us, revealing truth to us about ourselves and the true condition of our heart. The condition of our hearts as human beings is revealed in the Bible when it states, *"The heart is deceitful above all things and desperately wicked, who can know it?"* (Jer. 17:9). The point is you do not know your own heart and it will lie to you and deceive you. Only the Lord, who has true judgment and discernment about what is inside you, can reveal this.

> **The heart is deceitful above all things, and desperately wicked: who can know it? I the Lord search the heart, I try the reins,** *even to give every man according to his ways, and according to the fruit of his doings* (Jeremiah 17:9-10).

These judgments from Him are true and righteous, and specifically about us, even though we may not understand them at the time. Now let me tell you about another Person in the Godhead who helps to give us freedom and removes these veils from our hearts.

The Holy Spirit Gives Us Freedom From Veils

The Importance of the Work and Person of the Holy Spirit in Removing Veils from Our Hearts and Faces

> *Nevertheless* **when it shall turn to the Lord, the vail shall be taken away. Now the Lord is that Spirit: and where the Spirit of the Lord is, there is liberty. But we all, with open face beholding** *as in a glass the glory of the Lord,* **are changed** *into the same image from glory to glory,* **even as by the Spirit of the Lord** (2 Corinthians 3:16-18).

The work and Person of the Holy Spirit are so important in our lives when it comes to this subject of removing veils from our heart, since He is the One who guides and leads us into all truth. Yes, truth is the key element to revealing the veils that cover the wickedness in our hearts that we cannot see. As the Bible states, our heart is desperately wicked, and the Lord asks who can know it? He then answers His own question: *"I the Lord search the heart, and I try the reins"* (see Jer. 17:10). It is the Lord who removes these veils from our heart and who in turn exposes and reveals the deceitful, hidden secrets and lies about the true condition of our character. In the book of Second Corinthians, Paul further explains that *"When it* [the heart] *shall turn to the Lord, the vail shall be taken away"* (see 2 Cor. 3:16). Again, it is the Lord who takes these veils away. But here in these passages of Scripture you must understand which part of the Godhead the Scripture is referring to. It plainly says, *"Now the Lord is that Spirit: and where the Spirit of the Lord is there is liberty"* (2 Cor. 3:17). So it is the Holy Spirit who helps and gives us freedom from these veils on our hearts that blind us to the truth. It also says this about the work and person of the Holy Spirit: *"For the fruit of the Spirit is in all goodness, righteousness and truth; proving what is acceptable unto the Lord"* (Eph. 5:9-10). It also says that He, the Holy Spirit, has no fellowship with the unfruitful works of darkness in our lives (known sin or unknown sin), but He instead reproves or corrects it. This means He reveals the darkness that is in our lives by the light of His presence. Early on in my walk with the Lord, I had a glorious experience when the Holy Spirit appeared to me. From this visitation I saw how important the work of the Holy Spirit is in our lives because He helps us overcome sin. The Bible tells us that the Holy Spirit works with and through us as our partner to put away the evil deeds of our flesh.

The Holy Spirit Appears to Me in a Dream

An Experience I Had With the Holy Spirit

In 1993 I had a dream in which the Holy Spirit appeared to me face to face. Some of you may initially have a problem with this type of appearance theologically. Consider, however, that the Father appeared to Moses, Israel, Daniel, Ezekiel, Isaiah, and the Apostle John on the isle of Patmos. And Jesus, His Son, appeared to men also. What makes you think that the Holy Spirit cannot appear in His bodily form to men? The whole Godhead has appeared to men at some time or another. I had this dream and the Holy Spirit appeared to me when I was a young Christian who was battling against sin and temptation during my singleness.

The Holy Spirit Disarms the Power of Sin in Our Lives and Removes the Veils

In this dream I saw the Holy Spirit stand in front of me. He said nothing Himself, but a voice from Heaven spoke saying, *"It is the Holy Spirit who neutralizes sin."* I knew this was the voice of the Lord Jesus. I had become familiar with the voice of Jesus and knew it was Him speaking while the Holy Spirit stood there quietly.

I wondered for years after this dream why the Holy Spirit stood in front of me, very much alive, but did not speak and had Jesus speak on His behalf. Years later I learned why by studying God's word. Jesus taught us about the Holy Spirit when He said, *"He will not speak of Himself"* (John 16:13). Jesus plainly said, *"... he shall not speak of himself; but whatsoever he shall hear, that shall he speak: and he will shew you things to come"* **(John 16:13).** This also means He will not personally speak about Himself. Just think; you can't find anywhere in Scripture where the Holy Spirit talked about Himself. Whenever the Holy Spirit is mentioned, Father God and Jesus are the ones speaking about Him. I'm not saying that the Holy Spirit does not talk; He just doesn't talk about Himself.

I Saw His Feathers and Wings but He had the Body or Form of a Person

The Holy Spirit stood right in front of me. He was the purest white that I had ever seen. His clothes and robe were white. His face, hands, feet and all of Him was the purest white—you can't even imagine—it was a white that is not humanly comprehensible! This is the strange thing though: He looked like He had the form and image of a normal man, a lot like Jesus when He has appeared to me, but He also had huge, beautiful, white wings as a part of His form. Also, the Holy Spirit had an all white body. When I've seen Jesus, He had on the white robe and clothes but His face had color to it. Jesus' body and face is not pure white all over. Jesus has color to his skin and has an olive complexion. This was the only time the Holy Spirit has appeared to me in a dream, and I have not seen anything like this since. In this dream He just stood there in front of me, alive and as beautiful as ever, with energetic and lively wings that moved gently as this voice from Heaven spoke to me!

The Holy Spirit Does Have Wings

He shall cover thee with his feathers, and under his wings shalt thou trust (Psalm 91:4).

The Bible is clear when it mentions the Lord having wings. But more specifically, you never hear people who have had an encounter with the Father or Jesus describe either of them as having wings. These two personalities of the Godhead do not have wings. The only person who saw wings on one of the bodies of the Godhead was John the Baptist when he saw the Holy Spirit as a dove (see

Mark 1:10). This is amazing! Because when it says throughout the Old Testament that the Lord had wings, it was really talking about the Holy Spirit. Only the Holy Spirit is described as having wings, not the Father or Jesus. Angels were created in the image of God because they have wings.

We were also created in God's image: "*...Let Us make man in our image, after our likeness*" (Gen. 1:26). We were created in the image of God the Father and Jesus, body and soul wise, and our spirits were made in the likeness of the Holy Spirit's image, internally, which the Bible mentions that can fly, soar, or travel at a fast speed. Remember the Spirit bears witness with our spirit, not our body or soul. This is the realm that the Holy Spirit resides in because our spirits are the part of us that the Holy Spirit created and is a reflection of Him; this is how we are created in the image of all parts of the Godhead.

It took me years to understand that this was an appearance from the Holy Spirit and to find Scripture to understand this visitation fully. There's only one man according to Scripture that was given the ability and privilege from God to physically see the Holy Ghost, and his experience matched mine. It was John the Baptist. John the Baptist's special assignment from God was to identify Jesus with the Holy Spirit's help, to testify that Jesus was the Son of God, and to point people to Him as the Messiah in this fashion. John the Baptist's special assignment from God was to identify that Jesus was the Son of God and to point people to Him as the Messiah.

The presence of the Holy Spirit was the premiere sign that God gave John to identify Jesus as the Messiah. God told John: "*That whosoever you see My Spirit descending upon and remaining this is He*" (John 1:33). That is exactly what happened when John baptized Jesus at the Jordan River. John physically saw the Holy Spirit appear and said, "*I saw the Spirit descending from Heaven*" (John 1:32). The Bible records that the Holy Spirit descended upon Jesus in the bodily shape of a dove. He was not a dove, but He had the bodily shape or form and features of a dove. The Holy Spirit is God and a person, not a bird. The Scriptures record that when John the Baptist saw him in the physical realm he talked about the Holy Spirit's body form and shape.

> *And the Holy Ghost descended in a bodily shape like a dove upon him, and a voice came from heaven, which said, Thou art my beloved Son; in thee I am well pleased* (Luke 3:22).

His face, hands, and body were white in color. He is not a dove but He has the bodily features of a dove. The Holy Spirit has wings even though He's a person! He is the purest white all over His body that you have ever seen! Now when Jesus appears He does not have wings. His glorified bodily shape does not look like a dove and He does not have wings. Jesus has the full stature and bodily image of a man.

The Holy Spirit's Appearance

The word appearance, which comes from the Greek word *phaneros*, means to appear.[1] It also means to reveal one's true character, the opposite of appearing in a false disguise or without disclosing who they really are. This is what Jesus was doing every time He came to me. The word appearance also comes from the Greek word *eidos*, which means "that which strikes the eye, that which is exposed to view."[2] *Eidos* describes a visible form or shape and this word is used to describe the Holy Spirit when He took bodily form as a dove.

Sanctifying Jesus in Your Eyes

"Woe Is Me for I Am Undone...for My Eyes Have Seen the King"

> *Then said I, Woe is me! for I am undone; because I am a man of unclean lips, and I dwell in the midst of a people of unclean lips: for mine eyes have seen the King, the LORD of hosts* (Isaiah 6:5).

There were many areas in which I had become more like the Lord, but there were still a lot of areas that needed work. When I compared my failures, weaknesses, and faults with the face-to-face visitations I had had, I saw over the years how much I was not like Him. Initially, I didn't understand or see this, but as I matured I saw the Lord more, and I began to respond like Isaiah did when he saw the glory of the Lord. *"Woe is me, for I am undone"* (Isa. 6:8). I saw how my character was flawed even after my conversion in 1989. I saw who He was, and then I saw who I was...

I saw how humble and low-key He was. I realized that we had different priorities. He valued what I had decided was insignificant, unimportant, and unworthy of my time—the simple things in life. I saw how my ways were nothing like His ways. Yes, I knew and believed that by faith I was the righteousness of God in Him, but in all honesty there were still so many attitudes and character issues that needed reforming. And, oh did He reform them!

After years of being slow and dull–minded, I began to notice and pick up that He was considerate on a deeper level of people, situations, and things that I had not been. Out of ignorance, my level of consideration for people and situations was so dull and not thoughtful in comparison. He was so meek, gentle, soft, mild-mannered, and tenderhearted, but I was so harsh and hard. He was so merciful, full of pity, and showed kindness to me as well as others who deserved nothing but judgment for our actions. I had the nerve to be judgmental, critical of others, and impatient—the total opposite of His nature. Years later I've wondered to myself, *"How could I have been like that?"* I demanded so much from others, that they relate to God and me in a certain way, when He didn't even treat me this way. He drew me with loving-kindness and gentleness! I didn't realize that I was like this until I saw Him as He is.

He accepted me the way I was and allowed me to come to Him that way, but loved me enough to not leave me the way I was. I was forceful to others, but He gently nudged me. He was low maintenance, but I was high maintenance. He made it so easy to be in relationship with Him and to love Him. I began to see how I made it so hard in many ways for people to get along with and be in relationship with me. Many of us have been this way in ignorance, and it takes us seeing Him to recognize how much we are not like Him. How ignorant I was to this and didn't know it! Although I was having all these visitations from the Lord, I didn't catch on to this until much later. He made it easy and I made it hard. I made it hard for people to maintain a relationship with me by having high, lofty, and pompous standards. At times it may have been the truth or in the name of God; it may have looked right but according to His character it wasn't. The majority of the church is like this today!

They emphasize one level of God's truth at the expense of another. I wondered, *"How does He maintain balance with all this?"* For instance, we are harsh about some forms of righteousness and holiness in God while forgetting to show mercy and grace in others. This makes us unhealthy, not well rounded, and out of God's order. God is first full of grace and then full of truth. I saw how I was out of order and had it all backwards. I was full of His truth but only had a little bit of grace and it ranked second in my life. I thought I was helping people by preaching and telling them the truth. I discovered through His more excellent way that I wasn't helping them at all. Truth is knowledge, but grace is empowering help. *Grace* means "giving assistance, favor, or divine empowerment to help bring about a change."[3] I saw that I was preaching the knowledge and truth of God's word, but that I lacked the grace in assisting and helping people to live the truth I preached.

He's Full of Grace and Truth

Remember that the Bible says that Jesus is *"full of grace and truth"*—not only the truth, but He is full of grace, then truth (see John 1:14). In other words, He starts by giving us divine assistance and help and then gives us the truth or knowledge afterward. He doesn't try to teach or push rules down our throat without first giving us the divine assistance to live them. Wow! Notice that Jesus died on the cross to help us before He required us to live by the truth that His death bought. Even the Father sent the Holy Ghost to enable us to walk out His statutes (see Ezek. 36:27). I practiced the exact opposite principles out of ignorance. At times I demanded that people obey the gospel of truth even before they had received the help and capability that Jesus promises to give!

I was unbalanced because I had grown up unbalanced in Him. Although I was being used by God powerfully in miracles and prophecy and was a blessing to thousands under His anointing, I still lacked so much in these areas. I thought I was helping people and thought I was full of grace. Many preachers fall into this deception like I did. We minister to people and see godly fruit and think that is where the real root of our character is, but it's not. When we are under the anointing and being used by God, it's really more of Him and not so much of us.

I didn't understand that how I treat people after a service and how I live my life outside the pulpit is what means most to God. The heart and ability I have to bless people outside the pulpit is real proof of the level of my personal character. The proof of the grace we possess is in our ability to lovingly help and assist others.

Our character should be proven in many areas with people so that we are wholesome and well rounded in all things. This is the character of God and the level of integrity that He lives by. He neither demands that we live a certain way, nor does He condemn us when we don't. Rather, He gives us His divine power and ability to become like Him in the ways we lack.

I saw this truth unfold in Scripture and when I saw Him face to face. He shared Himself. The Lord shares His glory, power, nature, ability and His name (character) with us unselfishly and without insecurity. There were times when I shared only a little about myself and what He had given me with others because of my own insecurity. I was hard on my sons and daughters in ministry when they fell short in character or maturity. Then I realized that He promoted me even though I had failed His standards miserably. He promoted me in the midst of my failures. I was not like this with others. The Lord used what I called failure in my life and turned it into what we call success. I didn't know how to display this grace to others and to promote individuals without demanding that they pass a test. I thought that this was the way He is. God does promote us when we pass His test, and He does demote us when we fail, but He doesn't do this all the time. The Bible says that He will not always scold us: *"He will not always chide"* (Ps. 103:9). I realized that I demoted others and myself when we didn't pass a test, but that He didn't treat people this way. Oh, how awesome He is as God and Friend! And even after I had missed all of this, He still called me His friend. He was so full of love that I didn't comprehend it at that time. I could feel, smell, touch, and experience His love but how was I to become loving like Him?

Being Transparent and Free!

I was quickly falling miserably short! Have you ever been here? But in His compassion He replied to me with loving-tenderness and put my heart to rest by saying, *"I'm not asking you to work in becoming like Me in your own effort, but I'm asking you to enter into my rest, abide in Me, and let Me live My life through you!"* I had been so full of my own lustful desires and selfishness, but He is so unselfishly focused on me, seeking my best interests. I felt competitive with others in ministry at times. But Jesus made it about others. He makes sure that His followers come into the same victory His Father gave Him. I was so competitive and wanted to be on top, but He is so secure and at peace; He is not striving to get ahead. I saw how very jealous, envious, and competitive I was when new people were raised up to the scene before I was. How do you respond when people are promoted above you or before you? What are your actions and responses especially when you feel you should be promoted ahead of them? Does jealousy, competition, or envy grab hold of you? Do you strive to prove yourself during these moments? Do you pitch fits, have an attitude, and get disgruntled? The Lord had to reveal to me His divine purpose for raising multiple men up; He uses each one to bring something He desires on to the scene.

He had to show me the importance of each one of my brothers and sisters and His purpose for allowing them to come to the forefront. I got this way because I felt overlooked, rejected, belittled, and esteemed as the least. Later I understood that if I did not have pride, I wouldn't have been offended or affected by it. Those who possess true humility do not have to come to grips with being treated as the least, because those with true humility know and believe that they are already the least. Those who are truly humble feel at home when they are treated as the least in the Kingdom, because they embrace that they are the least. I saw how much I promoted myself in pride, but when I looked at Him, I realized He was not trying to earn a reputation.

I have never seen Jesus promote Himself in any encounter I have had with Him or in any place in Scripture. Jesus didn't promote himself even after He rose from the grave and was promoted to the right hand of the Father. He has never done what I was doing. I wondered why Jesus would tell people good things about me when I had messed up horribly and had many areas of my life that were falling apart. He gave me a simple answer: *"Love...Love... Love covers a multitude of faults."* He covered mine. He is always a loyal and loving Friend.

He suggested when I commanded. He commanded when I demanded. I was so lost and out of sync with Him. How was I ever going to become more like Him? By faith. Yes, one of the answers is by faith. By faith in the righteousness that God brought through Christ Jesus. He was so patient, tolerant, forbearing, and longsuffering with me. I was so very impatient with life, others, and myself. I was hasty, rushed, pushy, and I lived by striving, aggression, and anxiety. Let me stop here and ask you, beloved child of God, if you can identify with me. It's only when we become transparent that we become free. For years I covered my faults and sins. I struggled with being transparent in the Church for fear of being ostracized. I didn't see transparency in His body, because church members would often assassinate each other's character for it.

When I stood in front of the Lord, however, I knew that I could be transparent with Him about everything. Today I'm transparent and free, even in the things of God. He taught me that what I had observed in the Church was not His way of doing things! He showed me how much I am not like Him just so He could reveal how much He still personally loved me the way I was. He loved me beyond what any human being had. For He loved and accepted me for the person I was! While I was struggling with my weaknesses, He said to me, *"I know what you are feeling, and I alone can set you free from your shame. I allowed you to see, experience, and feel all these things about yourself to show you your need for Me and ultimately to reveal My love to you. I love you beyond the incomplete knowledge and understanding you have of yourself. You will never really fully know how much I love you until you cross over into eternal life."*

I didn't feel condemned around Him even though I knew He commanded righteousness. Most of us, even those in the Church, know that in this life love is conditional and given only until someone sees the worst in us. People reveal their hate for us when they see the worst part of us. *"It's the opposite with Me,"* the Lord said. *"I use the revelation of how much you are not like Me, exposing all your weaknesses, flaws, and shortcomings to show you how deeply I love you."* Then He said, *"I love you, David. Tell My people how much I love them beyond any right or wrong they can do or have done. I simply love them. Tell them that I will use their weakness and flaws to reveal My love for them."* He shared this revelation with me and then He left.

After I Saw Him, My Face Began to Literally Shine

Your Face Will Also Shine When You See His Face

Supernatural things started happening very soon after the Lord removed the veils from my face. I attended college in Charleston, South Carolina, and became friends with a wonderful family who took me under their wing while I was away from home. One of the daughters in this family, Jackie Shaffer, became a good friend to me and is a powerful evangelist and pastor today. Together we attended the Victory Church of God in Christ church that was founded and pastored by Robert Coaxman. Pastor Coaxman was 93 years old when I first met him, and he had a spiritually thriving and anointed congregation of people who were full of love, light, and power.

As a young man, I spent a lot of time seeking the Lord, and one day Jackie said to me, *"David, you remind me of this man of God that I've been reading about lately: Benny Hinn."* At this time in my life I had never heard of Benny Hinn. She said, *"When this man was younger, around your age, He also spent a vast number of hours with the Lord and lived the same type of consecrated life."* She had been reading his book *Good Morning, Holy Spirit*.[4] She said to me, *"You need to get this book I've been reading; I believe it will help encourage you!"* And oh it did! Little did she know that it would not only encourage me, it would revolutionize my life from that moment on and introduce me to a relationship with the person of the Holy Spirit that I never knew existed at that time! I bought the book, *Good Morning Holy Spirit* by Benny Hinn, in 1991. When I picked it up, I could not put it down. Tears began streaming down my face while reading the first few pages.

There is a revolutionary moment in the book where Benny describes a Kathryn Kuhlman service he was in where he saw the glory of God. I had always been fascinated with Moses and the cloud of glory that God allowed to follow His ministry. The story about Moses' face shining like a light bulb after spending time with God on the mountain always intrigued me.

Until I had read Benny Hinn's book, I had only heard this type of experience talked about as a relic of the past occurring during the time of Moses. Even though I had seen the Lord in a dream two years before this, and I knew that everything written in the Bible is real for today, I had never heard of anyone in this dispensation walking in what Moses walked in with God. The biblical account of Moses was awesome to me, but you have to understand that I wasn't taught to expect these types of things as I had been raised in a Baptist Church. As I read Pastor Benn's description of the service and about the blessing he received while there, everything in me began to cry out: *"I want this! This is what I've been looking for."*

He saw a cloud of glory envelop and surround Kathryn Kuhlman while her face was shining like a light bulb through the mist of His glory. Pastor Benny thought his eyes were playing tricks on him at first, but then realized that they weren't. As I read his book, everything in my whole being screamed out, *"I have to have that!"* At that time I didn't quite know how to articulate my hunger; I just knew I wanted God like that inside me and on my life! I said to myself, *"I've got to have God's glory, the Lord, surrounding me and inside me in that dimension and in that way."* So right at that moment I put the book down and said to the Lord, *"I want this!"*

I was in college at the time and living in an apartment-style dorm that wasn't like regular college dorms. I was a student at Johnson and Wales University studying to become a chef! So even though I had to live with other college students, there was extra space in the house and nicely sized closets. I went inside the closet in my room to fast and pray for three days and to ask the Lord to give me what Kathryn Kuhlman had walked in! One of my college roommates thought I was weird for locking myself up and not coming out of the closet for three days. During this three-day period I prayed to the Lord and asked Him to give me whatever it was that Kathryn Kuhlman had that I had just read about in Benny Hinn's book. I prayed, I sang, and I worshiped the Lord until I heard His voice on the second day. He said to me: *"Praise me for it; I have already given it to you; just praise Me for it during the rest of your fast."* After I heard His voice, I obeyed.

From Thursday to Saturday I didn't have any classes so I used that time to praise Him. After the three days ended, I came out of the closet and went to sleep in my bed for the first time since the beginning of the three-day fast. When I came out, I didn't feel any different. I didn't feel an overwhelming power or a cloud all around me. I just believed what the Lord said to me!

I must share with you what happened next to confirm the seriousness that God had answered my prayer with. The morning following my fast, we had a glorious service at Victory COGIC. For the 7 P.M. evening service we were scheduled to join another church that was located a few hours away. The church asked if I would drive members of the congregation to this service in the church van. I was happy to do it. I enjoyed serving and doing whatever I could do to bless God's work and His house. When we arrived, we discovered that the guest speaker didn't show up to speak at the service. So, without any notice, they asked me to preach! The only thing that was on my heart to share was what God had shown me about America in a dream during the three-day fast. So I preached the message God gave me from this dream! After the service, Sister Jackie Schaffer came up and told me that she had seen the whole service in a dream the night before. In her dream I was asked to preach unexpectedly at the church we were visiting, and she saw me pacing the pulpit like I normally do when I'm preaching about something very important that needs to be heard. She said to me, "But the strange thing is that in the dream you paced the floor, walking back and forth, and a cloud of glory and mist surrounded you, and your face was shining through the cloud!"

I began to weep and feel the anointing as she told me this dream she had seen the night before. It was God using her to confirm the promise He had given me on the fast—the cloud of glory around me and inside me. She had no idea that I was seeking God for this and had just come off a three-day fast for it, because I didn't tell anyone about this fast. I did it in secret! Then she said to me, "While you were preaching today, I observed everything that I saw in the dream happening." Then she said, *"And I also saw that cloud of glory around you, and your face was shining like a light bulb!"*

God will use other people in your life by giving them dreams to confirm His destiny, purpose, and will for your life. He will put these people around you and speak to them in dreams so that He can relay a message to you! This same thing happened when the Lord spoke to Gideon through someone else's dream to encourage him that he would be victorious in battle. Gideon overheard someone in the enemy camp of the Midianites who dreamed that Gideon was victorious over them. This confirmed and encouraged Gideon that the Lord promised to give him victory. As I continued to seek the Lord in deep prayer and communion, these face-to-face experiences with Jesus continued, and glorious things started happening to me. This noticeable manifestation of God's presence was beginning to manifest openly before other people. I had first experienced it several months earlier after encountering the Lord in a vision with a waterfall. This story is in my first book. This trip to Rhode Island was the first time that I was manifesting God's glory in an open way.

After the service in which Jackie Shaffer pointed out that I was glowing, it happened again in front of many more people. I didn't know it would happen, but as I was teaching a Bible study to about 20-30 people on the university campus, my hands, face, and skin began to glow like a physical neon light. This happened in front of everyone with no warning! As I was teaching the Word of God, I started to glow and shine and the people in this class noticed with great amazement and astonishment. They came up to me and said with wonder, "You're glowing; you're shining!" I didn't feel anything different at the time; I didn't even realize I was shining until 30 people started telling me so all at the same time. I know the Lord didn't do this to bring glory to me, but to testify of His power and glory. The glory of Moses' countenance was a direct result of his face-to-face relationship with the Lord. His face shone like a light bulb because the Lord's countenance glows like the sun (see 2 Cor. 3:7; Rev. 1:16). Moses' face was just a reflection or mirror of the glory he experienced and saw from God. Your face will also shine as you have this face-to-face experience with Jesus. This is real for today!

It Happened at Captain D's

This was not the only time this happened in college. It kept happening at different times when I least expected it. I came home from college for a visit in 1993. At the time, I was working with a church in Memphis, Tennessee that was in great revival. My mother dropped me off at this church, and I stayed for three days to fast, pray, and spend quality time alone with the Lord. After three days,

MY TRIP TO HEAVEN

MY TRIP TO HEAVEN

my mother came to pick me up. When I came out, I noticed that she was looking at me strangely. My mother has always helped keep me from getting prideful about my relationship with the Lord, so she didn't say anything to me about what she saw. I asked her to take me to Captain D's for some fish because I was hungry. She agreed but told me that she had to stop at a clothing store first. As we walked in, the cashier and customers began looking strangely at me too.

Then a few of them started saying: *"Look at his face. It's glowing; it's shining."* My mother replied: *"Yes, he just got done being shut away in prayer."* Then we left the store and went on to Captain D's. We were standing in line because there were quite a few people there and everyone started looking at me with strange expressions again. My mother saw all of this. I heard someone say that I was shining. I didn't realize this was taking place on my face. I didn't feel any different! As I sat down to eat, the man that was sitting in front of us was just staring uncontrollably at me while we ate our food. I remember my mother also telling these people that I had just come out of an extended prayer time. I don't know if they understood her comment or not, because my mind was focused on getting something to eat! I know wanting to get something to eat may sound carnal, but I *didn't know* the Glory of God back then like I do today! You also will shine like a light bulb in the physical realm, not just the spiritual realm, as you spend time in the Lord's presence.

Like Moses you will come out of the Lord's presence with a shining face. I've never forgotten these experiences, even though I didn't understand the value of them back then. All I know is that I asked God to let me experience the glory cloud that surrounded Kathryn Kuhlman, and for my face to shine like hers did. I look back now, and it was powerful. A few years ago someone on my staff and another person came to me after I preached a message and said that my face was shining as I preached about the Kingdom of God. Now, there are people who are with me continuously and know this does not happen all the time, but they take notice when it does. Someone told me one day after my prayer time: *"David, I see the Lord in your eyes."* I'm so humbled by what the Lord has done in my life, and I don't ever want to lose this work He has done. I know that all this has happened as a result of this face-to-face relationship with the Lord. Your face will begin to shine too! God doesn't just want to anoint you from head to toe, but He also wants to cover your body, face, and skin with His glory!

It Happens Again

About a year later the same experience happened again in Charleston, South Carolina. I was staying with a wonderful pastor who loved the Lord.

Stay Out of the Mirror

As I was walking around the house one day, I went to the bathroom to wash my hands. When I looked up at my face in the mirror, I saw what people were talking about for the first time. I was shining and glowing. My face was magnificent, even to me, and was covered with the glory of God. It was so beautiful. It was such a physical manifestation that I started putting my hands on my face to feel and touch my skin to examine it. I didn't feel any different. I felt the same. No overwhelming power—nothing! I was just glowing with the glory and presence of God. All of a sudden this pastor walked by and saw me looking at myself in the mirror and being fascinated by what was happening to me. He spoke to me with great firmness and authority, *"Get out of the mirror!"* Then he continued, *"With that type of anointing on your life, you cannot look at yourself. Stay out of the mirror!"* I didn't understand the revelation of what he was telling me until years later, but from that point on, I knew something unusual was happening to me. When I go to a special place to be with the Lord for a few days, I put a towel on all the mirrors in the room. Believe me, when you are walking in the glory of God, you follow different rules than when you walked in His anointing or in the gifts of the Spirit.

Chapter 3

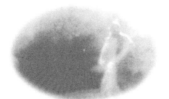

FACE-TO-FACE MEETING WITH JESUS AT THE MERCY SEAT OF CHRIST

"Learning How to Desire Judgment From the Lord"

AS OUR RELATIONSHIP continued to grow, I began to learn that we are to desire the Lord's judgment.

> *...the judgments of the Lord are true and righteous altogether. More to be desired are they than gold...* (Psalm 19:9-10).

Every year I began to ask the Lord to inspect me, to judge me so that I could walk and serve Him more perfectly. I also asked Him to give me an extra, personal face-to-face visitation each year after I received the inspection from Him. You really need to understand the season I was in at this time. I had grown in the Word and had come to learn three major things about walking with the Lord in this love relationship. First, The Lord loves those He disciplines.

> *For whom the Lord loveth whom He chasteneth...* (Hebrews 12:6).

Jesus said this when He appeared to John on the island of Patmos concerning the condition of His Church:

> *As many as I love, I rebuke and chasten…* (Revelation 3:19).

So I had come to understand and embrace the fact that being rebuked and corrected concerning my faults, failures, and errors was just a part of a normal, intimate, love experience with Jesus. In the natural realm, being corrected doesn't feel like love the way encouragement does. We receive encouragement as a form of love, while being ignorant to and sometimes resentful of the same love that manifests itself in correction, discipline, and through rebukes. You never hear Jesus saying in the Bible, *"I love those whom I encourage,"* but He does say, *"I love those whom I chasten."* Amazing! This is very opposite to our nature and understanding!

Second, I learned that we need to ask to be inspected by the Lord. In his book, *Plans, Purpose, and Pursuits,* Kenneth E. Hagin Sr. relates a face-to-face encounter he had with Jesus. Jesus told Pastor Hagin, through a mild rebuke, that he had pastored outside of God's will for twenty years. Pastor Hagin replied to Jesus by asking, *"Why did you allow me to pastor outside your will for so long without telling me?"* Jesus replied back to him saying, **"Because you never asked me."**[1] True judgment from the Lord requires that we yearn and ask to be inspected. This is what you call "seeking His righteousness." This not only implies seeking and doing what is right, but doing what is right in the right way.

Third, I learned from Rick Joyner's book, *The Final Quest,* that we should ask and yearn for the judgments of God as they allow us to serve Him more perfectly and to walk with Him more intimately.[2] I was already experiencing the judgments and corrections of God as I had asked him much earlier in my walk to inspect me in our face-to-face visits. These books helped me to interpret what the

Lord was already doing in my life and what process He had started in me. In the second and third chapters of the book of Revelations, three of the seven churches experience inspections and judgments from the Lord. After learning about the importance of the judgments of God, I asked Him to inspect me every year so that I would stay current in my relationship with Him.

Appearing at the Judgment Seat of Christ

*For we **must all appear before the judgment seat of Christ***; *that every one may receive the things done in his body, according to that he hath done, whether it be good or bad* (2 Corinthians 5:10.)

He Treated Me Like a Son

In 1997, the Lord appeared to me several times and inspected my life and corrected me concerning many things including our morning times together. You can read more about these in my first book, *Face-to-Face Appearances From Jesus*. At the end of this season, He appeared to me again to summarize the things he was correcting me about. Although it may sound like He only appeared to reveal what I had done wrong, He did also appear to reward me for what I had done right. During one of these face-to-face visitations, He said that I was faithful enough to be entrusted with the keys of the Kingdom. It meant everything to me that He mentioned the things I had done right and that He could promote me in. He also showed me that I have a right-hand place in His kingdom. I share more details about this promotion in my first book, *Face-to-Face Appearances From Jesus*, and later on in this book. In this face-to-face visit, I was off into a deep sleep once my head hit the pillow. All of a sudden, I was sucked out of my body at the speed of light and was in Heaven. At the time I didn't understand this type of experience like I do now. All I knew then is that I appeared in Heaven and stood in a line of people at the Judgment Seat in front of Christ.

Appearances From Us to Jesus

The Lord Not Only Appears to Us, but He Also Requires Us to Appear Before Him

Appearances don't just mean that the Lord comes from Heaven to visit us, but they also mean that we will appear before Him. David knew this principle and longed for it. Not just for the Lord to appear to him but he longed to appear before God! It says,

> *My soul thirsteth for God, for the living God: when shall I come and appear before God?* (Psalm 42:2).

You see, we must not only be hungry for Jesus to appear to us, but we must have a hunger to appear before Him as well. There are times, seasons, and occasions that He requires us to appear before Him. The Lord has been scheduling appointments for us to appear before Him since the beginning. Even in the Old Testament the Lord made a requirement for His people to appear before Him every year (see Deut. 16:16; 31:11; 1 Sam. 1:22). The Bible also records that He wanted the angels and people to present themselves before Him (see Rom. 12:1; Exod. 24:1-3; Job 1:1-8). Even Jesus had to appear before the presence of God and could not allow Mary to touch Him before He presented His body as first fruits before the Lord (see John 20:16-17; Heb. 9:24-28). The Bible also says that when it comes to the Judgment Seat of Christ we must appear before it.

The Judgment Seat doesn't come to us, but we must appear before it; this is what happened to me in this visitation appearance. Jesus didn't appear to me, but I appeared before Him at the Judgment Seat of Christ. Before I knew what was happening, I was standing involuntarily in front of Him. At the blink of an eye, He will summon us to appear before Him and we will return with no time lapsed. When we stand before Him, our spirit is separated from our body and we are either in the spirit realm or in Heaven. But when He appears to us, He is visiting the earth. The only time that we can voluntarily appear before God in this realm, without being supernaturally summoned by Him, is by entering His presence through our prayer, praise, and worship. When we go into prayer and fasting to get into God's presence, we are appearing before the Lord.

How often do you appear before the Lord? The Lord instructed the Israelites to not come into His presence empty-handed and without a sacrificial offering (see Exod. 23:15; 34:20). When we come before Him through singing and worshipping, we are offering a sacrifice of praise (see Heb. 13:15). The Bible records that we are required to appear before the Lord for different reasons. One reason, as I've already mentioned, is for this inspection at the Judgment Seat of Christ. The Bible also mentions that we are to present our lives and bodies as a living sacrifice before the Lord. There are many additional reasons that we appear before the Lord, but these two are given so you can understand that it is not just about the Lord appearing before us but it is also about us appearing before Him!

The Visitation at His Seat

On this particular trip, I didn't get to look around Heaven or to talk with others like I experienced on another trip that I will tell you about later in this book. On this particular trip, I was only there so that Jesus could talk to me personally and so that I could be inspected. I was in one room in Heaven, and the room was pure white and glowing with glory all around. Later, I found out that this room was home to the Judgment Seat of Christ! I don't know how He does this—all I know is that it happens. I was immediately beamed up and brought to appear before the Judgment Seat of Christ where I stood in line with nine or ten other people who had asked to be judged by Jesus because of this same revelation. I knew that these people were still alive and were visiting from earth for this same inspection. Jesus was at the front of this line of people, and He looked very royal and dazzling in His white royal attire. He looked different to me compared to other times I had seen Him.

Jesus Sits in His Seat of Judgment in Heaven

He was sitting in this little seat that didn't look like a throne with armrests on the side, but rather like a small chair. The chair was also a little lower to the ground than a normal chair would be. I noticed this right away because Jesus was sitting lower than you would expect Him because of the short height of this little chair. While studying the Scriptures, I learned that Jesus was given His own Kingdom and sat on a throne in His own kingdom within His Father's Empire.

> *And I appoint unto you a kingdom, as my Father hath appointed unto me* (Luke 22:29).

I saw Jesus sitting at the right hand of the Father in a holy city in the Father's empire. The Bible never says Jesus was enthroned at the right hand of God; it says He was enthroned. God sits on a seat of authority on a throne within His heavenly city, and Jesus sits in a royal seat next to the Father at His right hand. Jerusalem is God's Heavenly city. This is the city we sing about in worship songs.

> *...the city of the living God, the Heavenly Jerusalem* (Hebrews 12:22).

Jesus does not have authority over God in this city, but He is the mediator and intercessor who sits at God's right hand in the mercy seat.

> *And to Jesus the mediator...* (Hebrews 12:24).

To understand this concept of kingdoms and empires better, consider the Roman Empire. During the Roman Empire, Rome ruled over many kingdoms around the world even though they had their own kings who sat on their own thrones. Rome itself was called the Imperial City because it was from this city that the empire ruled and governed the entire world. The government of Heaven is set up in a similar way. God is the emperor over the whole empire and the city of Jerusalem in Heaven is His city. It is the central city where His seat of Authority is located. Initially, I didn't understand this because I always saw or thought that Jesus sat on a throne at the right hand of God.

> *To him that overcometh will I grant to sit with me in my throne...* (Revelation 3:21).

This was a distorted view I had because of my upbringing, which emphasized that Jesus was always exalted; there was little mention or teaching of God the Father and who He was in relationship to Jesus. Now I understand that it was the Father that exalted Jesus and raised Him up to sit at His own right hand in heavenly places.

> *...when He raised Him from the dead, and set Him at His own right hand in the heavenly places* (Ephesians 1:20).

Americans often miss that there is godly hierarchy in Heaven among the Godhead even though they are One. Even Jesus spoke of this saying, *"...my Father is greater than I"* (John 14:28). The Bible says that all things have been put under Jesus' feet except

God. Some refer to the Scripture that says, *"I and my Father are one,"* to explain that the Father and Son are equal in rank (see John 10:30). Jesus didn't mean they were the same in rank or authority. Otherwise He would not have said, *"My Father is greater than I."* Jesus has been rightfully exalted by the Father, but He is not deserving of more glory than God, even though it is through Jesus that mankind comes to the Father.

...no man cometh unto the Father, but by me (John 14:6).

And there came a voice out of the cloud, saying, This is my beloved Son: hear him (Luke 9:35).

The Church has not taught about the hierarchy of Heaven without putting a damper on the promotion and honor Jesus received by obeying the Father and going to the cross for our sins. After my trip to Heaven, I found Scriptures that record that Jesus was "seated" at the right hand of God, not that He was "enthroned" at the right hand of God. Jesus does have a throne, but when He sits next to God it is not on a throne. It is a little seat. This seat is what we read about in Scripture called the *Mercy Seat* (see Exod. 25:22). He promised to commune with us from the Judgment Seat of Christ, and the Bible says the saints will stand before Him here. You can be judged at this seat early in your walk or later on in it (see 1 Tim. 5:24-25). This judgment seat of Christ is not the same as the Great White Throne Judgment that the Bible speaks about in Revelation 20:11-15, which John the apostle saw while on the island of Patmos. Christ's judgment is a merciful one and saves you from the Father's judgment that is pronounced from His great, white throne. These are two different forms of judgments spoken of in Heaven.

The Judgment Seat of Christ deals with Christ judging His sheep—His saints, the saved—according to the deeds done in this body and life and includes receiving rewards for the good things we have done. These rewards are the mercy part of the judgment! We enter eternal life with these rewards. The Great White Throne Judgment is the time when the dead—small and great alike—shall stand before the Father. During this judgment, all are judged according to their works and based upon whether their names are written in the book of life (see Rev. 20:11-15). There is a seat at the right hand of the throne of God.

He Was Judge

Jesus was sitting down and facing us. He looked more serious and loving than I had ever seen Him look. The best way I can describe it is to say that He had a very important look on His face in that moment. As we stood in front of Him in a single-file line He told the first person, *"You made it,"* and then that person moved to the side. The next person moved up in line, and Jesus said, *"You didn't make it,"* and the person would move out of line while the next person would move up in front of Jesus. There wasn't a sense of the wrong type of fear. There was a great reverence in that holy place. I knew in my heart that when He said "You made it," He was approving us to move to the next level in our walk and ministry with Him. The line kept moving forward, and He continued like this until He got to me. He was still sitting in His seat when He said to me, *"You didn't make it."* My heart dropped! I didn't understand. With bewilderment I then asked Him, *"Why, Lord, didn't I make it?"*

Judgment Filtered Through Mercy

"He Got Up From His Seat as Judge and Talked to Me as a Friend"

With this He arose from His chair and took me to a separate room in Heaven by myself so that we were alone like intimate friends. He

93

spent special time explaining the reason for His judgment so that I would understand. I felt so greatly honored by the King of kings. I noticed that He didn't take anyone else aside to speak with them and explain why they didn't make it. I also noticed He never got up off His seat to stand until I asked Him this question. I felt honored. When we arrived in this separate room, He sat down and began to tell me the reason I didn't make it saying, *"Because you didn't study your word long enough."* Then I replied with defensiveness, but also with great reverence to Jesus saying, "Lord, but how was I to know?" I honestly didn't know, but there was no excuse. Then Jesus replied to me with great love. His reply was with tenderness, eyes full of fire, and firmness, but He spoke more gently than I had ever heard Him speak when He corrected me face-to-face. He said, *"You can find out what you really want to know."* Years later, I realized that I didn't study His Word long enough because the anointing and gift of revelation on my life as a prophet blinded me from having the heart to really search out His word thoroughly enough.

I made the mistake of not studying like I should have because, like a lot of prophets, I relied on the anointing and the gift of revelation as I ministered. As I preached the Word of God, the anointing brought the people great revelation, but it also ministered to me as well. I lived off the inspirational word, the *rhema* that was preached through me by the Spirit instead of really studying myself.

> *...as the same anointing teacheth you of all things, and is truth, and is no lie, and even as it hath taught you, ye shall abide in him* (1 John 2:27).

I neglected studying for my personal foundational growth and building of character. You see, as prophets and ministers we can preach on a level we ourselves have not been promoted to yet. God allows this because it's Him working through us to give His people what they need and each person is on a different level. Our preaching can be on a higher level than where we personally live spiritually. This is possible because Jesus said, *"Lord I thank You that You have hid these things from the wise and prudent and have revealed them even unto babes"* (see Luke 10:21). God can reveal great revelations to babes and even allow them to preach. This still doesn't make them an adult in their walk with God. This is where most young ministers (like I was at the time) get deceived because they mistake the level of revelation and preaching that is being manifested to them and through them for maturity.

Sadly to say, even mature Christians get blinded by this same deception and think an immature convert or minister is more mature than they really are because of their gifting. So as a result of this, I thought I was doing enough study and didn't know I was not studying long enough. This is what allowing the Lord to judge you does for you. The Lord's judgment inspects you and shows you the areas you are lacking and falling short in as a Christian or as one of His students. Right after my conversion I would study for too long, and the Lord had to shut my Bible for me and make me go to bed. I wondered how I could have gone from that extreme to not studying long enough. Again, for years I didn't understand how important this visitation was from Jesus.

I also saw Jesus' personality expressed and that He doesn't like excuses. He then revealed to me that He would give me over to satan as a result of this error in my life. At that moment I felt like, *"Lord, why are you judging me so harshly?"* I thought *"Lord, I just didn't study Your word long enough."* Over the years I searched the Scripture and discovered that this was a grave offense and more serious than I had understood at the time.

Also, I had asked the Lord to judge me ruthlessly a year earlier. He replied to me, ***"David, you asked me to judge you ruthlessly so that you could serve me more perfectly! If I didn't, you would be like so many of My servants and people who go on without having these assessments until they die!"*** Then I thought, *"Thank*

You, Lord!" His judgments are to be desired, but they didn't feel good! No. Not at all. I hadn't realized that preachers are judged by a different standard especially if they are a special messenger or have an apostolic voice! I didn't understand for years why He would allow me to be delivered over to satan. In the next chapter I will share Scriptures that explain why God gives us over to satan for trials. But at the time I thought, *"Lord, what love is in this? What purpose could there be in satan testing me?"* I thought, *"He will destroy me."* Then He said, *"I will allow him to come against you for a season and for you to be delivered into his hands."* Then Jesus said to me, *"This will be satan himself, not a prince demon or regular evil spirit."*

Honestly, when I first heard Jesus explain this to me, I was silently offended in my heart. Out of love and respect for who He is, I said nothing to Him about it, but I was hurt. I didn't understand the doctrine of authority and what it meant to be delivered over to satan's hands. I thought, "Am I a bad person?" I hesitated to include this teaching in this book because I knew that some may misunderstand it and have a negative reaction to it leading to my persecution. In addition, I haven't always had the wisdom of Scripture and the ability to articulate how wonderful and what an honor it is for the Lord to deliver us over to satan for His purposes and not the devil's. Years later, I have come to understand that this process of being delivered over to satan for a season is one of the greatest expressions of love and privilege that He could give a man on earth. You may be wondering, like I did, "Why?" I'll explain why in the next few pages and in the following chapter. For the next seven years, my life was a violent battle and trial with the enemy of my soul and it wasn't until this season was complete that I began to get revelation on these things.

Jesus Does Not Accept Excuses

And they all with one consent began to make excuse (Luke 14:18).

Jesus mentions in one of His parables that He invited people to His banquet, but people replied with excuses in response. The Lord Jesus does not accept illegitimate excuses from us. He's loving and understanding, but He's firm in the conviction of our study of His word. I also learned that He could not approve me for the next level of relationship and ministry, no matter how close I was to Him, at this point of my walk. Most saints don't understand this—Jesus cannot pass you to your next level with Him if you do not study to show yourself approved unto Him.

Speed Up—Study

The Importance of Studying the Lord's Word

Study to shew thyself approved unto God (2 Timothy 2:15).

If ye continue in my word, then ye are my disciples indeed (John 8:31).

The word for *study* in this context comes from the Greek word *spoudaz, which means, "To use speed."* This implies us moving at a fast and accelerated pace, making an earnest effort, and endeavoring and laboring to become acceptable and approved to God through studying His word. In this context, this word *spoudaz* also means "To make it ones aim, striving ambitiously to be well pleasing, acceptable in His sight and current with the Lord after assayal, trial or test."[3] I was dull of hearing, like the Bible says, because of a lack of studying God's word. I had been slothful in the business of studying His word.

Slow people are described in the Bible as being *"dull of hearing,"* and they are slow to catch on to spiritual truths because they are not up to speed about a subject through study.

> *Of whom we have many things to say, and hard to be uttered, seeing ye are dull of hearing* (Hebrews 5:11).

For the most part, you can't talk to these dull hearing people about things on a deep level because they are lagging behind in their hearing of God's word through studying. The Lord is the same way. Throughout life, He is always trying to teach us things through other people we encounter each day, as well as through trials, circumstances, dreams, visions, and so forth. Because we are so slow and lagging behind in hearing and studying His word, He has to say to us, just like He said to the apostles, **"I have many things to say unto you, but ye cannot bear them now" (John 16:12).** Paul said the same thing in Hebrews, *"Of whom we have many things to say, and hard to be uttered"* (Heb. 5:11). In all actuality, you are lagging behind in being able to catch on to what we want to say about this subject because of your lack of study!

This is the importance of studying the Lord's word—so that we will be able to understand and quickly catch on when He is speaking to us in any way and through any person while receiving His message with total enlightenment. It didn't have to take me over fifteen years to comprehend the revelation about slothfulness that He was trying to reveal to me in a dream. But because of my lack of study and research of His Word, I was dull in comprehending or understanding fully what He was trying to say to me! The opposite of this is what the Bible describes as being of quick understanding. You see, this was one of the veils on my face that was hindering me from hearing the Lord with understanding and total comprehension. The Lord can appear to you, but you must look at Him with an open face. Every veil that is causing distortion of your view of the Lord has to be removed.

During this time I was not seeing clearly because I did not clearly understand. Truth helps to remove these veils. That's why Jesus admonished his disciples to continue in His word long enough saying, *"...If ye continue in my word then are ye my disciples indeed..."* (John 8:31). Then, on the next night He went on to say *"And ye shall know the truth, and the truth shall make you free"* (John 8:32). You see we are bound and not free in so many areas because of a lack of comprehending truth the way God does. When we study and continue in the Lord's word long enough by allowing the Holy Spirit to come upon our lives to teach us, He will reveal areas to us that we need present truth in. These truths will in turn remove those veils on our minds and hearts. Wow! When you understand this truth you will began to say what David, the psalmist, said, *"I will delight myself in thy statutes: I will not forget thy word"* (Ps. 119:16).

You see, when I first became a Christian, I loved meditating in the word day and night. It was wonderful to me, but I lacked zeal, warmth, and a deep level of interest in researching the Lord's word. I did not have the fervent desire to study intensely by dissecting every word in each passage to get the full understanding and meaning. I didn't even know that we were supposed to study God's Word in that way. I had never heard of researching the words of the Bible for their original Hebrew and Greek meanings. This was still an excuse like Jesus said. I had limited my study to just meditating on His Word, but I could have found out what I wanted to know if I had a heart that was interested enough in researching God's Word. Jesus was really talking about the condition of my heart.

I was "slow of heart" as a result of being "slow of hearing" the Lord's Word through studying. Remember, again this word *study* means in the Greek "to use speed." This is why the Lord wants us to study, so that we will not be lagging behind in our comprehension and understanding of Him in things. He wants us to be "up to speed" through study of His word. We must stay current with Him. If we are behind, we must "speed up" to catch up and on to what He's doing and saying!

Searching and researching the Word speeds you up. That's what Jesus meant when He said to me, "*You can find out what you whant to know.*" This is the area where I lacked. I meditated on the Lord's Word, which established a memory of the Word and a habit of doing the Word in my walk with God, but I lacked key, strategic information and revelation that I would have gained from researching the Word. I was a meditator but not a researcher. Researching is finding out knowledge. We can all find out what we want to know. Jesus was telling me there was a lack of zeal or desire to research. We must continue in His Word until the discipleship process is finished. I didn't study His Word long enough. The Word continuously deals with the amount of time you stay in the Word. How long do you continue in His Word? Until you show yourself to Him (not man) to be approved.

Study to the Point of Approval

You must study long enough until you are approved and graded as an A student by God. Jesus said that I hadn't made it because I didn't study His Word long enough to show myself approved.

Many study until the point that they learn information or revelation, but that's not necessarily enough Word in your life to cause you to mature in your ability to hear His voice or comprehend His truth. Some study to preach or to show that they can preach or break down a Scripture text. The point is to examine what you are studying to accomplish. If it's not to be a mature, seasoned believer who is able to discern the voice of God and to please Him with your hunger for the richness and stability of scriptural revelation, and to love and commune with Him through His Word, then your study is in vain and outside of God's conditions. It is unacceptable.

Many of us are studying the Word to the point that we gain knowledge, but we must not study merely for knowledge because without a deeper purpose it will lead to vanity and pride. As the Scripture says, knowledge puffs up, but love edifies (see 1 Cor. 8:1). We must first study to love and please God, then to edify ourselves for the purpose of being a blessing to others. We must study to love and fulfill the greatest commandment—to love the Lord our God with all our heart (see 1 John 2:5). Jesus said that if we love Him, we will keep His commandments. This is what studying to show ourselves approved is about. We study to fulfill the first and greatest commandment: to love the Lord.

The Importance of Searching the Lord's Word

Jesus Doesn't Want Us to Think, Suspect, or Suppose Our Theology

> *Search the Scriptures; for in them **ye think** you have eternal life: and they are they which testify of me* (John 5:39).

We don't search the Scripture thoroughly enough, and we go off half-cocked assuming we know the Lord's word deeply and intimately when we don't. We have our own definitions and interpretations of what many of the words in Scripture mean, and when we study them out we discover that they really don't mean what we thought they did. This is why Jesus admonished us and said, *"Search the scriptures; for in them **ye think** ye have eternal life: and they are they which testify of Me"* (John 5:39). The Scriptures in the Old and New Testaments testify of Jesus.

This is why it is paramount and of great importance that we know His Word. Jesus tells the Pharisees to go beyond reading and meditating on Scripture. He tells the Pharisees that they needed to search, which means in this context to *look it up*. This means we are to thoroughly search and research the Lord's Word with the help of the Holy Spirit so that we don't miss something and think we know it when we don't. I learned in my research that we also play a role and part in the salvation Jesus accomplished for us on the cross. Many think or suppose they are saved because they gave their lives to the Lord and accepted His blood shed for their sins. Yes, we are saved by grace through faith, but this was His part. The Bible admonishes us to work out our own salvation with fear and trembling.

He Places a High Value on His Word

Heaven and earth shall pass away, but my words shall never pass away (Matthew 24:35).

Not one jot or tittle shall pass from His word until all be fulfilled (see Matthew 5:18).

With this visitation He was also trying to teach me the importance of spending enough time studying, dissecting, and searching His word. In 1995, I was sleeping when I heard a voice saying, *"Study the gospels."* Then I woke up. I knew it was the Lord's voice, but I failed to really study deeply. I studied God's word some and experienced tremendous revelation from the Holy Spirit while I prepared sermons, but I didn't quite understand that I wasn't studying in a way that would cause me to learn the things I needed to learn for where He was taking me.

The Veils Exposed: Standing Before Him With an Open Face

But even until this day the veil was upon their heart (2 Corinthians 3:15).

Describing the Veils That Were on My Face, Mind, and Heart

One of my veils caused me to become unbalanced. The parts of the Lord that were very clear to me became the things I focused on, but this caused an imbalance in understanding other areas of His nature. For example, I had always said that Jesus required bold-ness like a lion to obey God. Then God appeared to me and told me that He was looking for a man to stand on the authority of His word. So I understood the authoritative, bold, aggressive, and aus-tere side of His nature. I concentrated on these things for years and neglected to study His meek and gentle side, which is also part of His character.

This veil deceived me, gave me an unbalanced view of Jesus, and caused me to deal with others in an unbalanced way. I would be the lion: bold, hard, firm, and authoritative when I should have been gentle, soft, and mild mannered with people in certain situations. Eighteen years ago Jesus appeared to me as a lion with a gold face. He then revealed to me that His lamb-like nature was required to completely drive the devil out of His temple, because His lion form or nature was too big. His lion nature could have served as a hindrance! I thanked the Lord for teaching me this. I thought to myself, *"Why didn't Jesus teach me these things plainly and a lot earlier? Why had He let so many years go by without voluntarily telling me? Why did I have to go through so much and make so many mistakes in the process by failing and messing up so badly?"* Well, here was my answer. The Lord will not do what you can do for yourself.

You **must** do your part. If you do not study, there are certain things He will never tell you. That's your part. Remember we are co-laborers with the Lord. I was behind, because I was not up to speed with the Lord. So I didn't understand the things He was trying to reveal to me until I did my part to study years later. I realized that all of this pain and suffering was caused by a lack of knowledge of the Word and was the result of being slothful.

Chapter 4

He Brings Me Into Sonship and Approval

"He Loves Those Whom He Chastens"

For whom the Lord loveth He chasteneth
(Hebrews 12:6).

The Revelation of Being Delivered Over to Satan

WHAT I LEARNED later put the icing on the cake and gave me greater understanding as to why Jesus delivered me over to satan for not studying the Lord's Word long enough. I was reading a book written by a great woman of God on deliverance. In this book, she teaches from the book of Second Timothy:

> *Study to shew thyself approved unto God, a workman that needeth not to be ashamed, rightly dividing the word of truth. But shun profane and vain babblings: for they will increase unto more ungodliness. And their word will eat as doth a canker: of whom is Hymenaeus and Philetus; Who concerning the truth have erred, saying that the resurrection is past already; and overthrow the faith of some.*

Nevertheless the foundation of God standeth sure, having this seal, The Lord knoweth them that are his. And, let every one that nameth the name of Christ depart from iniquity. But in a great house there are not only vessels of gold and of silver, but also of wood and of earth; and some to honour, and some to dishonor (2 Timothy 2:15-20).

Hymenaeus was preaching from God's word in error because he lacked in his study and said that the resurrection was already past causing the faith of some to be overthrown. By the Spirit, the Scripture records how Paul dealt with this man by delivering him over to satan:

This charge I commit unto thee, son Timothy, according to the prophecies which went before on thee, that thou by them mightest war a good warfare; Holding faith, and a good conscience; which some having put away concerning faith have made shipwreck: Of whom is Hymenaeus and Alexander; whom I have delivered unto Satan, that they may learn not to blaspheme (1 Timothy 1:18-20).

Paul called their lack of study and preaching of false doctrines blasphemy. Paul says that this deviation from truth and faith caused their salvation and deliverance to become diseased and eaten up like "a canker" which is the same disease known as gangrene. When I heard this teaching, I began to understand the gravity of studying God's word.

When we don't study God's word long enough we go off half-cocked and preach things in error. Depending on the severity of these errors, we can cause the precious faith of other believers and saints to be overthrown. God is displeased when we destroy or tamper with the faith of others. God values faith very highly. The Bible calls faith "precious" (see 2 Pet. 1:1). The Bible also says that the trial of faith is more precious than gold (see 1 Peter 1:7). In another place we hear Jesus saying, *"When the Son of man cometh, shall he find faith on the earth"* (Luke 18:8).

Faith is what Jesus looks for in us. Faith pleases Him. As teachers of the Word, we cannot hinder or disrupt the faith of others because it is so precious to God and is what He looks for in mankind. We are called to help build the faith of others, not to destroy it. Jesus prayed that Peter's faith wouldn't fail when satan attacked him to sift him as wheat. Jesus also said:

> *But whoso shall offend one of these little ones which believe in me, It were better for him that a millstone were hanged about his neck, and that he were drowned in the depth of the sea* (Matthew 18:6).

That is a harsh judgment, but Jesus values our faith highly and calls it precious. We also know that faith is directly linked to hearing the pure, unadulterated Word of God preached (see Rom. 10:17).

Delivered Over to Satan to Learn

> *...whom I have delivered over to Satan, that they may learn...* (1 Timothy 1:20).

When I began to see this in Scripture, I thought, *"How many preachers or saints go on without this divine, supernatural, revelatory teaching on the judgment of the Lord in their lives?"* I was hurt because I didn't ever want to err like these teachers who preached false doctrines because they didn't know the Word. The Lord was trying to prevent me from ultimately doing what they did. I wasn't preaching anything horribly wrong that was compromising the faith of the Saints like Hymenaeus and Philetus, but He was trying to teach me the principle that led to this horrible mishap in their lives and ministry. They were delivered over to satan. I know that this statement sounds horrific to many people. The Lord said to me, *"David, what you have to understand from the beginning of time, since man's conception on earth, is that I have been delivering My premiere servants over to satan for different purposes."* This doctrine of delivering men over to satan didn't just start in the New Testament with the apostles. I had only seen this revelation in Scripture when apostles delivered men over to satan for different reasons.

Paul delivered a man over to satan so that his flesh would be destroyed and his spirit saved (see 1 Cor. 5:5). He did this because the man would not repent of fornicating with his father's wife. The point is that Jesus revealed to me that this ministry of delivering men over to satan didn't start with his servants in the New Testament. They actually received this principle from God in the Old Testament. God has always used satan to accomplish His purposes, even when satan didn't know He was being used.

Job Was Delivered Over to Satan to Test His Integrity

Then the Lord began to give me examples of this in the Old Testament. He said, *"For example, take My servant Job. It was I who mentioned him to satan and who gave satan permission to touch Job and even for Job to be delivered into satan's hands."*

> *And the Lord said unto Satan, **Behold, all that he hath is in thy power...** (Job 1:12).*

> *And the Lord said unto Satan, **Behold, he is in thine hand...** (Job 2:6).*

The Bible tells us that God delivered Job over to satan because God was pleased with Job's integrity, not because Job had done anything wrong. Adam was delivered to satan after disobeying God's command. The Garden of Eden protected Adam just like Job had been protected before, and when he was sent from the garden this protection was removed.

Adam Was Delivered Over to Satan After Being Put Out of the Garden

Wow! One man was delivered over to satan because he had obeyed God and lived with integrity, while another man was delivered over to satan for disobeying and displeasing God. The Bible says, "*...death reigned from Adam to Moses...*" (Rom. 5:14). This means that Adam was subjected to and delivered over to the reigning power of death the very moment he sinned. God's sentence for Adam's disobedience was death, and He used the prince-demon of death to fulfill this judgment.

King David Was Delivered Over to Satan

Another servant was King David; the Lord delivered him over to satan not because David just wanted to do evil by numbering the people. The Lord's anger was kindled at Israel and he sent satan to provoke and move David to take a census!

> *And again the anger of the Lord was kindled against Israel, and he moved David against them to say, Go, number Israel and Judah* (2 Samuel 24:1).

> *And Satan stood up against Israel, and provoked David to number Israel* (1 Chronicles 21:1).

The Holy Spirit Delivers Jesus Over to Satan to Be Tempted by Him

Jesus said to me, *"David, the Holy Spirit delivered me over into the hands of satan to be tempted and tried by Him."* The Bible records this:

> *And Jesus being full of the Holy Ghost returned from the Jordan and was led by the Spirit [driven] into the wilderness, being forty days tempted of the devil....And the devil, taking Him up into a high mountain...* (Luke 4:1-2, 5).

Jesus was delivered over into satan's hands to be taken by him and tempted, but Jesus came out victoriously! (See Matthew 4:10-11.) Jesus also helped me be victorious when I was handed over to satan!

It was the Holy Spirit that delivered Jesus into the hands of satan to be tempted. Jesus also said to me, *"David, My Father delivered me over to satan and to death,"* (see Luke 22:3; John 13:27). Jesus said in Scripture that satan entered Judas Iscariot's heart and he betrayed Judas, *"into the hands of sinners"* (Matt. 26: 45).

The Father's Cup: Jesus Was Delivered Over to Satan for Mankind's Salvation

> *...the cup which My Father hath given Me shall I not drink it?* (John 18:11)

While the prince of this world was taking Him to be crucified, Jesus said, *"This is your hour and your power of darkness"* (Luke 22:53). Jesus was delivered over to the power of darkness at the point of crucifixion. Look at what was accomplished during that hour that Jesus was delivered over to satan—Salvation for the whole world!

Look at Job; he received twice as much after being tested! All I'm saying is that there are different reasons in the Old and New Testaments that men were delivered over to satan. God allows this to accomplish His purposes. Here are a few reasons:

- To save one's spirit—Salvation (see 1 Cor. 5:5).

- To discipline those who have erred in preaching false doctrines due to lack of study and consequently leading people away from pure faith in God (Hymenaeus and Alexander: see 1 Tim. 1:18-20).

- To prove a person has godly integrity (see Job 1:6-12; 2:1-7).

- Because of His anger and displeasure with Israel (see 2 Sam. 24; 1 Chron. 21).

- For deliverance and salvation from pride. (Paul was tormented by satan's messenger which is similar to being given over to satan himself. See 2 Cor. 12:7.)

- Because of the sin of incontinency in marriage (see 1 Cor. 7:5).

- Because of sin (unclean garments represent sin in Zechariah 3:1-4).

- Jesus allowed satan to tempt Peter but He prayed for the stability of Peter's faith and asked for a quick recovery (see Luke 22:32).

God Uses Satan in the Lives of His People

And the Lord said unto Satan, Behold, all that he hath is in thy power... (Job 1:12).

And the Lord said unto Satan, **Behold, he is in thine hand...** (Job 2:6).

As Christians we generally refer to the events of our lives as being influenced by either God or the devil, but through my study of Scripture and experiences with trials I have come to understand that our lives are influenced by both. God gets satan involved. Most people in the church don't understand this, but it was God who mentioned Job to satan. Satan was not thinking about Job. And it was God who released Job into the hand of satan to be tried, tempted, and tested. It was the Holy Spirit that drove Jesus into the wilderness to be tempted and delivered over into the hand of satan. The devil was not looking for Jesus. It was also the Father's pleasure to bruise Jesus. After Jesus was delivered into the hands of sinners, satan bruised Jesus through these men. And the list goes on. The point is that we must be able to see God's greater purpose for allowing us to be delivered over to Satan. It sounds like a hor-rific and terrible thing, but it is a blessing in disguise.

God Uses Satan for the Purpose of Salvation

To deliver such an one unto Satan...that the spirit may be saved... (1 Corinthians 5:5).

God uses satan to accomplish His purposes. Satan is also employed by God for the purpose of salvation. Many Scriptures speak to this. One example is the case of the young man in sexual sin that Paul delivered over to satan for the destruction of the flesh so that his spirit would be saved in the day of the visitation of the Lord Jesus Christ (see 1 Cor. 5:1-5). It's the same case with Joseph, the "king of dreams." After all the suffering God allowed satan to take him through, Joseph still ended up saving scores of people by the end of his life (see Gen. 45:4-8; 50:20). Jesus is our prime example of this. He was delivered over into the hands and power of satan to be crucified unto death. But Jesus provided salvation for the whole world through His death at the cross.

It's for Your Salvation, Not Your Destruction

When God allows satan to assault your life by sifting and devouring you, it is always ultimately for your salvation and preservation, not for your destruction. God's purpose is always life, love, and light. Satan's purpose is always death, hell, hate, destruction, and darkness. The Holy Spirit sent from God above will work with us like he works with Jesus by driving us into the wilderness to be tempted of the devil (see Luke 4:1-2).

God Uses Satan to Purify Our Lives From Sin

The prince of this world cometh and findeth nothing in me (John 14:30).

The Lord uses satan in our lives to purify us. God knows that satan's purpose is to come and see if he can find anything impure or of Himself in us. How can two walk together except when they walk in agreement? To walk with satan means there is something in us that's in agreement with Him or there's something like him in our heart and lives. The Holy Spirit drives us into a temptation by delivering us over to satan so that we may be purified as God's chosen and elect.

David was driven into the wilderness by the divine plan of God through the evil spirit that had come upon King Saul. It was God's plan to send David to the wilderness so that he could begin the training and purification process to become king. God used the evil spirit in Saul to accomplish this. All of God's servants had to go through this. Moses had to be driven into the wilderness to be cleansed after murdering an Egyptian. Abraham was driven out of his country and didn't know where he was going. Joshua, the high priest, was also opposed by satan because of his impurity.

> *And he shewed me Joshua the high priest standing before the angel of the Lord, and Satan standing at his right hand to resist him. And the Lord said unto Satan, The Lord rebuke thee, O Satan; even the Lord that hath chosen Jerusalem rebuke thee:* is not this a brand plucked out of the fire? *Now Joshua was clothed with filthy garments,* and stood before the angel (Zechariah 3:1-3).

This opposition causes our dirty, spiritual clothes to be changed so that we are clean. Jacob was also driven to run after tricking his brother Esau. Job was driven into the wilderness to be purified and so were many others. One of the main purposes that the Lord delivers us over to satan is so that our character will be inspected, tested, and tried. Jesus revealed that satan's main purpose is to see if there is anything in us that is not of God that he can use to his advantage.

Seeing God in Your Thick Darkness
"See God in It"

> *...Moses drew near unto the thick darkness where God was* (Exodus 20:21).

> *Then said Solomon, The Lord hath said that he would dwell in the thick darkness* (2 Chronicles 6:1).

The Bible says God is light and there is no darkness in Him at all. The Bible also says the Lord God promised to dwell in the thick darkness. He is light and there is no darkness inside of Him at all, but He does dwell in your thick darkness. Moses knew this because he drew near to the Lord knowing that He was inside of the thick darkness. The people didn't know God was there because they stood far away from the thick darkness. The Lord also wants you to draw near to Him inside of your thick darkness no matter how mysterious it is. In spite of how dark it gets in your life, God is there with you. This means that you must learn to see and find God in your darkness no matter how thick it is! You must also seek to know why God allowed you to enter the dark season.

The Purposes of the Lord

> *But his father and his mother knew not that it was of the Lord, that he sought an occasion* against the Philistines: for at that time the Philistines had dominion over Israel (Judges 14:4).

We get sidetracked, fail, and stumble when we focus on what is wrong (the darkness) instead of looking to God to instruct us (the light). We shouldn't focus on the darkness, but we should look for God in it so that we can see Him. It's important to discover God's strategy for allowing bad things to happen. You can find God and see Him in your thick darkness or in your darkest moment. The most important thing is understanding God's reason or hidden strategies in why He's allowing something to take place that seems so wrong and the opposite of what we know to be right. As long as we have our minds and sight focused on the darkness (satan, wrongs, the things that looks unrighteous) we fail and stumble. As Jesus said, *"The darkness blinds our eyes"* (see 1 John 2:11). Whenever we look more at the darkness than God, it blinds our eyes from seeing God's greater purpose for our lives in it. God wants to open your eyes in the darkness, not blind them. Samson's parents couldn't see God's purpose beyond the unrighteous act of taking an ungodly wife.

Let's look at Joseph's life. God gives him a dream in which Joseph sees his destiny of greatness. He tells his brothers, they get jealous (darkness), throw him in a pit to kill him, and then decide to sell him into Egypt. (See Genesis 37:27-29.) These were bad things that happened to Joseph and caused a season of darkness to fall on his life. But what were God's plans in these circumstances? Joseph was sent to a country that would eventually promote him to a great position of authority. He worked as a slave in an officer's house. This officer, Potiphar, was instrumental in sending Joseph into the path of the pharaoh who would promote him. That's awesome. That's light! Joseph was delivered over to a season of darkness in a pit and a prison just so that he could later be promoted to the position of second most powerful ruler of Egypt. God did similar things with Jesus, David, Peter, Paul, Job, and many others. All these men were delivered over to satan and experienced the darkest moments of their lives, but they also came out victoriously and God's purposes were accomplished.

The Rewards for Loving Him

All Things Work Together for Good in Our Life

> *And we know that all things work together for good **to them that love God...*** (Romans 8:28).

In conclusion, you must understand that God promises to work all things together for our good. Just believe something good is going to come out of your darkness. God dwells in it. Find Him. Understand Him and believe Him through it. His love for us brings it all together and causes even the darkest moments of our lives to all make sense. His love makes it all count...everything. He can turn anything into a miracle. What Great Love!

Understanding God's Love and Chastisement

As many as I love I rebuke and chasten... (Revelation 3:19).

It took me time to totally understand His judgments. I didn't know it, but I began to experience them when I was just a young Christian. This is one of the things that enabled me to walk closer and more precisely with Him. It didn't feel like it, but I was really experiencing the Love of Christ in a way that I had not totally realized. This caused me to feel safe and secure.

For whom the Lord loveth he chasteneth (Hebrews 12:6).

When He corrects us, we are receiving His love. I didn't realize that I was being accepted, not rejected, when He corrected me.

...and scourageth [beat] *every son whom he receiveth* (Hebrews 12:6).

I didn't know it, but at these times the Almighty God was receiving me! Initially I thought that God was rejecting me through these corrections, but then I began to understand His word after He personally explained this concept to me. David said of the judgments of the Lord:

...the judgments of the Lord are true and righteous altogether. More to be desired are they than gold, yea, than much fine gold: sweeter also than honey and the honeycomb. Moreover by them is thy servant warned: and in keeping of them there is great reward (Psalm 19:9-11).

I began to desire the judgments of the Lord. Through His judgments, the Lord can keep you from future and presumptuous sin. So I asked for His judgment. When God allows you to see into the future by these judgments it changes everything. The Lord notifies and shows us things to come so that we can be changed and altered before they arrive! There's security beyond description in the judgments of the Lord.

This started happening after I asked the Lord one day saying, "Lord I ask that you would judge me and show me the mistakes that I could potentially make in the future that I do not see right now." With this, I went about my normal day. Just days later, it started and it hasn't stopped even until this day. Let me give one such experience.

My Trip to Hell

Thou shalt beat him with the rod, and shalt deliver his soul from hell (Proverbs 23:14).

I fell asleep, and with no warning began to have an encounter. I was immediately taken into hell. I didn't understand why, but I was put into a pit reserved for those who are lost and without God. I saw many people were being tormented and tortured by fire. I was allowed to experience the same separation from God that everybody else did. I didn't understand why I was down there. I was saved; I loved God. Thoughts raced through my mind. I couldn't have died in my sleep and ended up in hell, could I? Why am I down here like this? I served God. I loved Him. Why would He allow me to be put down here like this?

Suddenly, I saw Jesus in the distance. He was entering hell. Boy, was I happy to see Him! He was wearing his customary, beautiful white robe. I thought that I was lost and totally separated from

118

Him forever. I saw Him making His way toward me. He stopped to talk to different people as He walked toward me. I was amazed that Jesus would even talk to sinners or those who did not make it to Heaven. I didn't hear or recognize what He was saying to individuals as He passed along, but I know He was speaking briefly with each of them.

When I saw Him doing this, I decided to ask Him why I was down in hell when He came to me. You see, I had just had wonderful fellowship with Him in a visitation, so I didn't understand why I was down in hell afterwards. When He finally got to me, I noticed that His white robe was glistening even brighter than I had ever seen it. When He came up to me I cried out, *"Lord, why am I down here?"*

Then He did something that I didn't understand for years. Jesus with loving, tender care reached down and picked me up like a baby and put me over His knees as He bent to sit down, like you would when disciplining and spanking a child. As a matter of fact, He laid me across His slightly bent knees and started taking His right bare hand and physically beating me with His hands saying, *"Because you were not a friendly evangelist."* He spanked me with his hands in rhythm with His words! Then, suddenly I woke up, and I was back in my body. My heart was pounding fast and my blood was racing; I had just been in hell and the terror of this encounter frightened me. I got out of bed because I was covered in perspiration, and I wondered what He meant. I was also very happy that I had not been left in hell.

The Revelation of the Lord's Love and Chastisement in Hell

Correction from God is not a sign that He rejects you, but that He accepts you. Some might experience a visitation like this and make the mistake of thinking the same way I did. I thought after

I woke up, "Why would I go to hell for not being a friendly evangelist?" I could have understood if it was a dream, but no, it was a face-to-face visitation from Jesus personally and these words came directly from Him, who is the faithful and true witness of Heaven. His words never lie. The Lord had to give me balance. I was being judged and chastened in the worst kind of way, but I had asked Jesus for this. Hearing all these rebukes made me insecure, but I didn't realize at the time that they were securing my future and salvation in the Lord to a greater degree. Jesus was trying to divert me from continuing to be an unfriendly evangelist in the future. He wanted me to instead be an evangelist who associates and is companionable with others. My personality tended toward being a loner where I did not associate and keep company with other people. The Lord was telling me that I must tend my relationships like a pastor tends a flock. I must rule or protect and have oversight over my relationships.

You see, the Bible says that chastisement *"shalt deliver his soul from hell"* (Prov. 23:14). We are His children. When God starts correcting and beating us, it's a good sign that He not only loves and accepts us but that our soul is being delivered from hell. At the time I didn't see all of this. The Bible says that if you love your child, you will give them beatings in the early stages of their life so that their soul will be delivered from hell.

At this time of my life these corrections felt more like beatings and scourging than regular rebukes! It was all to save me and keep me from presumptuous or future sins. The Lord allows us to see the future or what's to come because when we do, it changes everything. It changes the way things play out when we see what could happen if we don't start repenting, changing, and adjusting our lives to the correction. God's correction is always done in love and meant for a peaceable result in our lives and not for torment or destruction. It may not feel good at the time, but it will produce a harvest that we will be satisfied with afterwards!

He Really Does Love Those He Corrects

Through all of this, He was trying to teach me His ways and how to follow Him. I didn't understand it then like I do today. He was teaching me how much He is a disciplinarian and how important chastisement is in my life if I am going to be all that He wants me to be. I didn't realize it but these ruthless and severe corrections would be essential to prepare me to operate in a greater level of authority. These rebukes would be essential!

The fact that Jesus took me to hell and beat me showed me that His mercy was keeping me out of hell. How awesome! I didn't see my errors, but since this trip to hell, I have become the friendliest evangelist out on the road!

Jesus also allowed me to see satan when I was in hell. He is the darkest being I've ever seen. His eyes have the very expression of evil and darkness that seems to come from beyond this world. He is forever lost and there is no love, mercy, or kindness in his presence. I knew he wanted to ultimately destroy me, but the Lord would not permit it. I also knew that I would not return or make it through my darkest night without the Lord. Jesus also taught me spiritual warfare to use against satan during this time and how to bind him! Jesus' presence in hell defeated all the torment around me that I had been feeling. I knew I would be all right when I saw Him. So I held on to Jesus as tight and close as I could during this seven-year period. The Lord moved me on to victory after this vicious onslaught on my life. I noticed that satan didn't just use other people to come against me in a harsh manner, but he also strategically used the unsanctified things in my life against me. I survived. He tested Jesus in the same way.

> *...for the prince of this world cometh, and hath nothing in Me* (John 14:30).

Jesus brought me through this trial, and I love Him for it. This is what real friendship is about. Being loyal to a friend during their darkest times—not just during the times of sunshine! Jesus has been a loyal friend to me at these dark times in my life, even when I failed to do so toward Him.

Jesus Holds the Keys of Death and Hell and Uses Them Today as Spoils

I am He that liveth, and was dead...and have the keys of hell and of death (Revelation 1:18).

Jesus said to me that He uses the keys of hell and death as a spoil of war to win souls:

These keys are part of the spoils that I gained in My victory at the cross. I took these keys from satan and then used them to unlock all the spoils he had in hell, which were the souls of men. They were waiting on Me to release them. David and others that Scripture mentions were unlocked. David, satan is now under my employment. I alone have the keys to hell, to satan's kingdom, and to death; I use them the way that I see fit. I also took the crown of death that symbolizes death's reign after the fall of Adam. Now hell and death are under My command, and I employ them for my purposes, David. So I have authority over hell, and I take My servants there to teach them that hell is real. It is a valuable lesson to show them that hell is real and that I died on the cross to save them from this evil torment. Many souls will be saved as a result of the testimonies of those who have been to hell. David, I am still using the spoils of My cross that were gained over 2,000 years ago to bring salvation to a lost humanity. Tell people that hell is real, and that it is not the place that I created for my creation. Tell men that they must repent and receive My eternal life before they die. I charge you to tell them. Tell them I love them, and that I died to save them from this terrible destruction.

He Was a Father and Treated Me Like a Son

If ye endure chastening, God dealeth with you as with sons (Hebrews 12:7).

He Brings Me Into the Relationship of Sonship

For years, I loved Jesus intensely. I loved Him and endured His chastisement, and my passion didn't decrease for Him! When I would cool off toward Him, I pulled it together and continued to follow Him. The Lord dealt with me as a son. He matured me. I moved into sonship with Him by going through His judgments. Jesus dealt with me this whole time through appearances. He was preparing me to stand before the Father and endure His correction, and I did! So He moved me to the next level of relationship with Him beyond being a son and into knowing Him as a friend.

Jesus distinguished stages in His dealings and walk with us. There are transitional phrases He uses in Scripture to describe this:

All things are delivered unto Me of My Father: and no man knoweth the Son, but the Father; neither knoweth any man the Father, save the Son, and he to whomsoever the Son will reveal him (Matthew 11:27).

Jesus answered and said unto him, If a man love me, he will keep my words: and my Father will love him, and we will come unto him, and make our abode with him (John 14:23).

And in that day ye shall ask me nothing. Verily, verily, I say unto you, Whatsoever ye shall ask the Father in my name, he will give it you (John 16:23).

For the Father himself loveth you, because ye have loved me, and have believed that I came out from God (John 16:27).

Your relationship with the Godhead moves steadily in transitions from one to another.

His Refreshing Appearance of Love

In Spite of My Faults, He Told Me Love Makes Him Not Want to Do it Without Me

At the end of this sonship discipline and training, the Lord visited me. I'm in tears now as I share this next visitation with you. Jesus appeared to me in a dream after this time of discipline telling me the wonderful things He was about to accomplish through my life for His Kingdom and His people. I asked, "Lord why me? There are others who are well more qualified than I am. Plus, I've made so many mistakes through this process of sonship while being trained and chastened by you." He gently replied in a meek tone. I had never heard these words articulated before and they changed my life. He said to me, *"Love makes me not want to do it without you, David."* I did not expect a response from Jesus like this. I had never heard such words in my life like these, even after 20 years of walking with the Lord! All I could do was weep and cry after He made this statement. I had never heard words like these nor love expressed in this way...ever! At this point, I couldn't hold back the tears. A release of warm tears flowed down the sides of my cheeks. You see, because His judgment and chastisement towards me through this Sonship process was so severe, I began to have an unbalanced view of how the Lord felt about me. I also felt this way because of how leaders and pastors in the Body of Christ began to treat me after seeing my flaws, faults, and weaknesses. I thought in my human understanding that when Jesus delivered me over to satan, I was somehow not worthy to be who He called me to be, but I was wrong! This was not the case at all; it was the complete opposite.

Jesus continued explaining in this visitation. He said, *"A lot of people are not committed to you in this way. Once they achieve what they want or come into some money, an anointing, or gift that gives them fame or status, they use this to circumvent you or to discard you. They will even use your faults, weaknesses, failures, and sins as an excuse for why they forsake you, overlook you, or pass over you. If they could do it without you, they would."*

Jesus went on to say, *"But true love makes a person choose not to do it without you. It is not because they can't or don't have the power to do it without you, but because they love you. Love commits them to do it with you even though you may not be the best."*

These are the words our Lord spoke to me. Wow! Remember, He loves you. Because He loves you, He chooses not to get anybody else to do what He has specifically called you to do, even though you've made mistakes or have fallen short of His Glory at times. The same goes for you who are reading this now! He could do it without you, but He chooses not to because His love for you keeps Him committed to you! I received the greatest compliment and love expressed from the Lord at this moment. Can you imagine the Lord saying to you, *"I can't imagine doing it without you."* It's the same message from the beginning of this chapter given by Jesus to all of us, *"As many as I love, I rebuke and chasten"* (Rev. 3:19)

Jesus Entrusted Me With the Keys of the Kingdom

THE APPROVAL

Keys Given in a Face-to-Face Appearance From Jesus

And lo a voice from heaven, saying, **This is my beloved Son, in whom I am well pleased** (Matthew 3:17).

As my relationship with the Lord continued to grow, I noticed that there was a level of trust being built between the Lord and me. I didn't realize how much the Lord trusted me until the summer of 1997. I had made so many mistakes. Like many Christians, I did not understand the love of God nor His kindness beyond my weaknesses and failures. Most people believe that the Lord requires absolute perfection from us in order to have a close relationship on this face-to-face level, but that is not the case at all. As a matter of fact, it is the opposite. He is mercy.

The Lord does require us to live a holy and righteous life, but our relationship with Him is not based totally (I must say this with balance) on how righteous we are or can be, but because He is righteous. During the year of 1997, I had a series of visitations from the Lord after fasting for a long time and asking Him to judge and inspect me. The Bible says to, *"Seek ye the Lord while he may be found, call ye upon him while he is near"* (Isa. 55:6). Because, *"...ye shall seek me, and find me, when ye shall search for me with all your heart"* (Jer. 29:13).

When Jesus inspects us, His pattern is to encourage us first, and then to tell us the things we must change. He did this with the seven churches in the book of Revelations. In the summer of 1997, I went to sleep and I was immediately with Jesus. I don't know how He does that. I don't have all the answers, but I do know that when I fall asleep, He appears to me in dreams or comes to get me (in the body or out of the body). All I know is that I am with Him immediately after being summoned! I have been taken to various places and settings throughout the years. This time I was summoned to where Jesus was. He had on His customary, beautiful white robe.

He stood a little taller than me—about 6 feet—and was the perfect stature of a man. He had sandy brown hair that was parted neatly at the top of His head and draped down His head in waves to His shoulders. I stood at His right hand. He started walking and I followed Him.

I need to say this. I felt so thrilled to be walking next to Jesus again! It's like we just went on a walk together as friends. I also felt overwhelmed that I was able to walk alongside Him. It was an intimate moment and was one of the most special times I've ever had with Him in our face-to-face relationship. Nothing was said at this point. He was very quiet. He took a few paces in front of me, maybe 7 to 10 steps, and then He stopped. When I saw Him stop walking, I stopped.

As I looked into His eyes, I could see a level of trust I had not seen directed toward me before. His eyes were filled with so much love, as they always were when I saw him, but this time they were also mixed with trust. He called my name with the most loving and gentlest tone in His voice saying, *"David, I'm giving you the keys to the Kingdom of Heaven. Whatsoever you bind on Earth, I, Jesus, will back you up and whatsoever you loose I, the Lord Jesus, will back you up."* At this point I did not know what to say, so I actually said nothing. I just listened to His soft, still words. As Jesus spoke, I knew that He was talking about the same keys that He gave Peter as a result of recognizing who He was.

I believe real authority from Christ is released in our lives when we get a revelation of who Jesus is. This revelation of the Son of God causes us to be able to be trusted by Him in a special way with His authority. By this time, I had intensely walked with the Lord for seven full years. I had prayed and fasted for hundreds of hours. I felt so humbled that the King of the universe would come to me and entrust me with the keys to His whole Kingdom. I felt so inadequate and wondered what this message really meant. It has taken me years to understand the full ramification of power and authority that He gave me. But immediately following this visitation, I began to see whole regions change, revival break out in whole cities, and an increase of authority to command and decree God's governmental will and desire over regions and people. I didn't totally understand why Jesus would give me these keys to His Kingdom or what they were for until I studied the Scriptures. I didn't know how to use them. But in time, I would come to understand how to operate in the authority Jesus gave me. Jesus gave Peter alone the keys to the kingdom.

> *When Jesus came into the coasts of Caesarea Philippi, he asked his disciples, saying, Whom do men say that I the Son of man am? And they said, Some say that thou art John the Baptist: some, Elias; and others, Jeremias, or one of the prophets. He saith unto them,* **But whom say ye that I am? And Simon Peter answered and said, Thou art the Christ, the Son of the living God.** *And Jesus answered and said unto him, Blessed art thou, Simon Barjona: for flesh and blood hath not revealed it unto thee, but my Father which is in heaven. And I say also unto thee,* **That thou art Peter, and upon this rock I will build my church;** *and the gates of hell shall not prevail against it.* **And I will give unto thee the keys of the kingdom of heaven: and whatsoever thou shalt bind on earth shall be bound in heaven: and whatsoever**

thou shalt loose on earth shall be loosed in heaven
(Matthew 16:13-19).

If you notice the whole point in this passage started with Jesus asking them, *"Who do men say I am?"* Then He ended up asking, *"Who do **you** say that I am?"* None of the apostles could answer and give the revelation. None of them knew, except Peter who received a revelation of who Jesus was from the Father. We know this was Peter! He didn't get these keys from Jesus just because He was an apostle. He received these keys because he was given a revelation of who Jesus was as the Son of God, as the Messiah! The point is that Jesus gave him the keys after he had a revelation of who Jesus was! Great authority is released from the Lord in our lives when we come into an intimate knowledge of Jesus.

Suddenly the Holy Spirit showed me this in Scripture, and He began to cause me to reminisce and think back on what had happened in my life before Jesus entrusted me with these keys to His kingdom. Fellowship had erupted between us. I had an intimate and thorough knowledge of who He was. Suddenly, I realized He really did all this in my life just because of the relationship we had developed. It was based on nothing more and nothing less. The revelation of Jesus Christ in your life will cause Jesus to give you authority on the earth.

The Results of the Keys

Keys Are Released and Regions Are Transformed

After the Lord entrusted me with these keys, we began to see whole regions changed in America. One region was a place called Shaw, Mississippi. We saw a bar shut down and the mayor of that town was filled with the Holy Ghost! Not only that, but the whole jail and prison system there was totally put out of commission because there was no need for it. Masses of people gave their lives to the Lord. Oh how badly we need this in our metropolitan cities in America. Until this very day, the pastor who invited me there has told me that the bar owner who shut down his establishment and gave his life to the Lord during this revival is saved and the bar is still closed! They also have not been able to build the jail system or police station again. What power! This happened 10 to 11 years ago!

Brooklyn, Illinois, Transformed

Another such incident happened after these keys were given to me in Brooklyn, Illinois. The mayor heard that the Lord was beginning to transform regions through the ministry He gave me. She invited me to come and minister to her region in Brooklyn. We saw great things take place. The Lord told me to use the keys He has given me to loose wholeness and health in that region by speaking financial blessing on the economy and on the mayor. I turned to her and said, *"The Lord told me to loose 3 million dollars into your hand for this region."* At the same time, the Lord told me to speak judgment on the Mafia establishments in that area so that they would shut down their illegal operations. The Lord also said to loose the building of a new bridge from St. Louis over to this area. The old bridge was worn and torn down. The Mafia threatened to kill the mayor and our ministry team. They also threatened to frame the mayor for stealing money.

These Keys Caused the President of the United States to Fulfill Prophecy

Three months after I released this money to the mayor in 1999, President Bill Clinton went to Brooklyn to give the mayor three million dollars. Around the same time, many of the Mafia clubs and illegal establishments were completely shut down! In 2008 I went back to visit Brooklyn and met with a pastor who remembered the word I had given in 1999. He then told me that we were standing in one of the buildings that had belonged to the Mafia. I didn't know it, but he had turned one of the Mafia buildings into a church. Then he said, *"Everything God had you speak about Brooklyn nine years ago has come to pass. All those who sought your life to kill you are dead or in jail. Even the man who owned this building is in jail at this very moment. The Mafia did set the mayor up and accused her of stealing money, but the powers of darkness did not prevail!"* This was definitely the result of the authority released to me through these keys.

Whole Mental Hospitals Healed

After these miraculous regional transformations, the Lord kept doing mighty things. We were seeing people healed of tumors, blindness, being mute, being crippled, and other diseases. People got out of their wheelchairs when Jesus appeared in services. But He made a special and unexpected visit. I knew a young man who had a mental breakdown and was admitted into a mental hospital in St. Louis. I was very close to him, and I got word that he wanted me to come to the hospital and pray for him. So I went, but I didn't know that the most amazing thing was about to take place!

When I arrived at his room, I began praying for him along with some of the staff members I had brought with me. We prayed for him and commanded the illness to leave his mind. Mental illness is a difficult disease to heal and we do not see many healings. It is not hard for God, but it is hard for us. As we prayed for him, his mental sickness immediately and completely left him. He arose from the bed healed.

Jesus Appears in the Hospital and
Performs a Mass Miracle

Right after this man was healed, Jesus suddenly appeared to me and stood on the opposite side of the bed. His face was shining, and He was wearing His beautiful, brilliant white robe. He said to me: *"David, use the keys that I've given you to pray for healing in this whole mental hospital, and I am going to walk through this hospital and heal the people."* So I did. I didn't know that something this dramatic was going to happen. As we walked out of the hospital room with this healed young man who was ready to go home, scores of people started coming out of their rooms saying, *"We are healed… Our minds are free."* A stampede of patients came from other floors that we had not visited. It was uncontrollable, and the receptionist or nurse at the desk didn't know what to do. We told her, *"You need to release these people; they're healed."* Sadly, she told us that she wouldn't get a paycheck if all those people were emptied out of the hospital because they were healed.

How sad it is in America that the pharmaceutical companies hold people in bondage with medicine and drugs just so they can live off of other people's illnesses and subtly take advantage of them. This was a notable, mass miracle, and my whole staff, the doctors, and nurses were astonished! I didn't lay a hand on a single one! This was Jesus and He was demonstrating His power through the keys of the Kingdom.

Chapter 5

Jesus Begins Appearing Notably in Services, Cities, and Countries

"The Day of His Notable Appearances"

WE HAVE TO understand that we are living in the notable day of the Lord which the Bible speaks of.

> ...*before that great and notable day of the Lord come* (Acts 2:20).

The word notable comes from the Greek words, *epiphanes*[1] and *epiphanio* which mean "the memorable, known, and visible appearance." Did you hear that? We are living in the day that the Lord appears to us. This explains why the Lord is appearing to thousands of people on the Earth in visible face-to-face encounters, in dreams, in visions, and in broad daylight. The word notable describes something that is visibly seen to the naked eye. This explains also why the appearances of the Lord are happening in our generation.

Can a Nation Be Born Again in a Day?

Who hath heard such a thing? who hath seen such things?
Shall the earth be made to bring forth in one day? or shall
a nation be born at once? (Isaiah 66:8).

A few years ago, two majorly awesome events occurred in which people in Muslim countries encountered Jesus face to face. The first story made national news in Indonesia—the largest Muslim country in the world, One night, a man went to sleep and the Lord Jesus appeared to him and told him who He was saying, *"I am Jesus Christ and I died for your sins."* Jesus went on to tell this man additional things that led him to salvation. When this man woke up from the dream, he knew he had seen the real risen Lord and that Allah was not the true and living God. You must understand that in some Muslim countries these precious people can be killed for professing faith in Jesus Christ. So after he woke up, the news media reported that he went to a restaurant and started telling people about seeing Jesus in a dream the night before.

A Whole Nation Born Again in One Day

"Whole Muslim Country Saved Through Jesus Appearance"

Who hath heard such a thing? who hath seen such things?
Shall the earth be made to bring forth in one day? or shall
a nation be born at once? (Isaiah 66:8).

"Jesus Appears to Everyone by Night in the Whole Country"

As this man told others about his dream, they confirmed that they had also seen Jesus in a dream on the same night! I remember reading a news article about ten years ago reporting that Jesus visited everyone in this whole Muslim nation on the same night! The whole nation converted to Christianity in one night by the appearance of the Lord! Wow, now that's power. Yes, a nation can be born in a day! Jesus is now appearing to whole Muslim nations where the gospel is not accepted. Jesus, Himself, is evangelizing! We serve an awesome Lord!

Isn't this beautiful! Another incident happened along the same lines in a Muslim-majority, third-world nation that was just as tremendous. This is a true story and it also made international news and headlines. A young woman was killed in a tragic accident, leaving behind two beautiful and precious children. They were young and still under the age of 12. Her brother, uncle to her children, had to take them in after his sister died. He started getting impatient with the children as time went by, and he wasn't raising them properly. So being upset, he took them to a cemetery and buried them alive in two separate tombs. For two weeks or more, these children remained inside the tombs until someone heard and discovered them while walking nearby. When the news media got wind of the story, they were all over it to find out what had happened. They asked these two children how they survived for so long without food or water. You know little children can't go that long without eating! The amazing thing is that both of them answered the same way even though they were not buried together! You should also know that these children were raised Muslim and had never heard of Jesus!

Jesus Appears in This 21st Century and Feeds a Little Boy and Girl

They saw a fire of coals there, and fish laid thereon, and bread. Jesus saith unto them, Come and dine. Jesus then cometh, and taketh bread, and giveth them, and fish likewise. This is now the third time that Jesus shewed himself to his disciples, after that he was risen from the dead (see John 21:9,12-14).

Jesus Still Feeds People Today

They replied to the media saying, *"A man in a white robe—He said His name was Jesus from Nazareth—came and fed us everyday!"* Wow! Amazing! I wept when I first heard this. How awesome! What love and compassion. These children and their country will never forget about this experience; it changed a whole country! Jesus still appears to people, feeds them, and tells people that He is from His hometown Nazareth!

> *...they saw a fire of coals there, and fish laid thereon, and bread....****Jesus saith unto them, Come and dine.... Jesus then cometh, and taketh bread, and giveth them, and fish likewise. This is now the third time that Jesus shewed himself to his disciples, after that he was risen from the dead*** (John 21:9,12-14).

This is what America needs. This is what the world needs. And this is what our generation needs! The Lord began to tell me that He's going to visit and appear to America this way. The Lord is allowing these types of appearances to happen in the "notable" days of the Lord, which lead up to His grand appearance in the event called the Rapture! The Bible says, *"And the glory of the Lord shall be revealed, and all flesh shall see it together"* (Isa. 40:5)! When he comes on the clouds every eye shall see Him (see Rev. 1:7; 1 John 3:2-3; Matt. 24:30).

Jesus Appears to 200,000 Muslims in T.L. Osborn Crusade

> *...he was seen of above five hundred brethren at once* (1 Corinthians 15:6).

Who said He couldn't appear to this many people at one time? He did it yesterday, and He's doing it again today! To confirm that these types of visitations are happening, I will share another story that has inspired me for years! In 1956, T.L. Osborn was speaking at a meeting in Jakarta, Java before an audience of 200,000 Muslims. All of a sudden, Jesus appeared notably in a cloud over the crowd. Everyone saw His face and glory and gave their lives and hearts to Jesus! Tremendous! What makes this story more awesome is that photographers captured this appearance on film! You can see Jesus' face in these pictures! You can read more about this event and see these pictures in T.L. Osborn's book, *Healing the Sick.*[2] This is what America is about to experience and we are beginning to see small evidence of it!

The Next Movement of God in America

"His Son's Notable Appearance"

America Needs a Face-to-Face Encounter with Jesus

In America, we experienced a wave of healing and miracles from the 1940s to the 1960s. We are currently watching prophets walk in their amazing gifting. America has not yet experienced a move of God in which people begin to see Jesus appear to them face to face that defies the boundaries of the existing church experience. This is the next move of God in America, and He will openly show His face to our generation in these types of encounters. This will happen to whole metropolitan cities in America at one time. High officials, presidents, kings, governors, businessmen, the wealthy, the famous, the poor, and the unknown will see visions of Jesus. This is what all of America needs! We need a real revival that transcends our churches and will shake our world with undeniable evidence that is too great to be ignored by the world or pushed under the carpet as insignificant.

This next move will affirm to all who God is before the end comes. It will happen! America will be shaken through a visitation to all in our land. Jesus commissioned me to bring this message to our country. Everyone needs to prepare to meet with God in a face-to-face encounter. This is already happening on a small scale in our country, but many in America will soon have a face-to-face encounter with Jesus!

I have a special message to the preachers and pastors in America. Our gifts and anointed sermons have not opened up all of America to experience God the way that a nation-wide face-to-face appearance can. No matter how many people you have blessed or reached at this point, it is still only a small portion of America and the world. America has not experienced God in this way yet. I believe He can get more done in a short, face-to-face appearance than we can accomplish in a lifetime of ministry using our God-given gifting and anointing. The answer to the ails of our generation is just the reality of Jesus. Today men just want to experience God. They want to know if the God we serve is real. When Jesus appears, it dissolves all doubt.

We Cannot Change the World if We Have Not Been With Jesus Face to Face

These that have turned the world upside down are come hither also (Acts 17:6).

138

And they took knowledge of them, that they had been with Jesus (Acts 4:13).

During the establishment of the early church, government officials said of the apostles and believers that they had turned the world upside down. They had this ability and power because they had experienced a level of intimacy with Jesus through knowing him face to face that we do not have as a church today. We need a face to face relationship with Jesus to be effective in our day and to turn the world upside down.

> *Now when they saw the boldness of Peter and John, and perceived that they were unlearned and ignorant men, they marveled; and they took knowledge of them, that* **they had been with Jesus** *(Acts 4:13).*

> *And they went forth, and preached everywhere,* **the Lord working with them** *and confirming the word with signs following. Amen (Mark 16:20).*

> *For wherever two or three are gathered together in My name,* **there am I in the midst** *of them (Matthew 18:20).*

Jesus Begins Appearing to Other People I Know

Jesus started notability working with me personally in ministry by not only appearing to me but to others also. I'll never forget when this first started happening in 1996 in St. Louis, Missouri. I was praying in the office on a Saturday evening. As I was bowed over on a chair on my knees, Jesus suddenly came walking through the walls of the office building and stood in front of me. He started talking to me about some personal things, but then He went on to share that He wanted me to train a young man, who was about 16 years old, in the apostolic ministry. At this time I was overseeing a small church and the pastor of this local congregation had a very anointed family that was called to destiny in ministry. This young man was one of the teenagers in that family. Even though he was only a teenager, the Lord had a great call on his life. Jesus went on to say to me, *"I want you to begin his training for ministry for he is called to be an apostle."*

I took Jesus' words seriously because I know the prerequisites and requirements for being called to the office of the apostle. I responded to Jesus with inquiry but also with great honor saying, *"Lord, you must appear to him before I train him seeing that this is your requirement for true, authentic apostleship."* To my amazement, I was not rebuked by Jesus, but His response was refreshing. He replied, *"I know, David, and I'm going to appear to him tonight.* He went on saying, *"Tomorrow when you see him at the church you are to tell him everything I've told you."* Now, there are many like Paul, who was called to the apostleship from the womb, but even He mentioned that it was through the revelation of Jesus Christ. The word *revelation* in this context means, "manifestation or appearance."

> ...the gospel which was preached of me is not after man. **For I neither received it of man, neither was I taught it, but by the revelation of Jesus Christ** (Galatians 1:11-12).

Well, after the service was over that Sunday morning, I walked up to the young man, greeted him, and began telling him what the Lord had said to me concerning him. Then at the end told I finally said, *"Jesus told me He would appear to you last night...Did He?"* He opened his mouth in amazement saying, *"Yes, I saw Him in a dream this morning in my sleep."* How awesome! From that point I began training this young man in the apostolic office and ministry.

Summer 1996

When I caught on to what Jesus was doing, that He would literally appear to the men who were working with me in this notable fashion, something went off in me. I began to realize how this could change the world and the lives of these men. I know that my life changed when Jesus initially visited me and I experienced Him for the first time in a real way. I began to realize that this was revolutionary! So, I started using my faith in this area to believe the Lord to work with me in a personal way with people as I witnessed to them. At this same church that I oversaw, I led a witnessing campaign to the surrounding neighborhood. I gathered the pastor of the church and his members and led them to the streets of their community to witness. Before we started out, I led the team on a three-day fast asking the Lord to appear to the people we would meet on the streets. I asked if He would appear to them on the night before in dreams or while awake in visions to prepare them to receive our witness of Him.

To my amazement, Jesus appeared to a number of people the night before we went out. He had answered our prayers! I met one unsaved man who started telling me that Jesus appeared to him in a dream the night before and told him to receive Him as his Lord and Savior. He began explaining this to me, not knowing that I had prayed and fasted for this very thing. It was so encouraging, and I was elated! How awesome this was! How powerful to have the Lord working with us in our witness for Him. I knew this was special, and I didn't let up on the pursuit of this awesome manifestation. This is what the Bible records happened with the apostles. They turned the world upside down because they had been with Jesus (see Acts 4:13; Acts 17:6).

These appearances didn't stop. He began appearing to my staff, and even confirmed to others through visitations that they were to join the ministry.

Cleveland, Ohio, 1998

It was 1998 and the ministry was growing during this awesome season. I was introduced to a great man, Bishop McKinney, and his wife Shirley, whom people affectionately called "Lady Bishop." They invited me to Cleveland to conduct a set of revival services. In these services, we saw the Lord do awesome things and demonstrate glorious and great power. One night the glory of God came in during intimate worship. It was so heavy that I could not minister. It was so thick that all I could do was sit down on the podium steps. We had seen many dramatic miracles and awesome displays of God's power, but this night was very special.

As I sat down on the steps, the people were still standing in the Lord's presence, and all of a sudden Jesus appeared in front of me in the middle aisle. He smiled at me. I noticed Him when I sat down (for the service was out of my control anyway). He then appeared and started taking over the service completely. We must learn to yield more completely as ministers and move out of the Lord's way! As Jesus stood there, I told the people that He was in the room, and I narrated what He was doing.

I could tell that a few people didn't believe what I was saying. The church I was ministering in has an incredible worship team and has a lively congregation that is always ready for a move of God, so it may have been visitors that did not believe Jesus was there. After Jesus smiled at me, He turned to walk to the back of the audience and said, *"Some of them don't believe you when you said that I'm here on the earth and in this service with them in my glorified body."* There were about 1200 people in the service that night. As Jesus walked, I narrated His every move to the people. I told them that He was walking toward the back. When He got to the end of the last pew, He turned left and walked to the farthest end of the last pew.

Jesus Appears and Heals a Young Man With AIDS

Because I was sitting down and the people were standing, I could not see Him in the back of the church at this point, but I could still hear Him. Then suddenly He began speaking to me saying, *"David, there is a young man who is a homosexual on the back pew. He came here to be healed because he has AIDS."* Now you have to understand that the service and atmosphere were charged with electricity and God's presence through awesome worship. Jesus then continued and said, *"David, I have My hands on this young man's shoulders and he feels electricity going through his body because I'm healing him of AIDS and setting him free from homosexuality. Tell what I'm doing openly and call this out."* I didn't know there was a homosexual in our audience or where he was sitting until Jesus turned left and pointed him out to me. Jesus said, *"The people will believe you more—that I am personally in the room—when you narrate this and tell it openly."* Then I said it! I shared everything that Jesus had told me about the young man. I shared that God was healing him of AIDS and delivering him from homosexuality, and I pointed to him in the back of the church.

Then I said to the young man, *"Come up here."* I was still sitting down. When the young man got up and came out of the back pew, he was trembling and shaking uncontrollably because of the power and electricity flowing through his body. I knew that this man was the homosexual that God told me about because he was the only one who came up to the front. Immediately, Jesus said to me, *"David, do not lay hands on him; just point from where you are sitting."* He was about 30 to 40 feet away from where I was sitting. As He walked down the middle aisle alone, I did what Jesus said and I pointed my index finger at him. I felt and saw a bolt of lightning and electricity flow out from my finger and hit him. The power of God raised him up about 6 feet in midair and threw him so that he was flying backwards through the air. When he landed on the floor slain under the power of God, he was completely set free from homosexuality and healed of AIDS. That's glorious power! The people saw this take place. The whole audience made an astonishing sound together: Whooo! They knew Jesus was personally there in the building when they saw this manifestation.

It Was Complete Glory

Jesus then came back down the center aisle again, passed in front of me, and stood at my left side. He looked at me and said, *"David, even after this there are still some that don't believe I'm here. Have all those who are skeptics come up here to where I am standing."* I had already narrated that Jesus had walked up to the front so then I said, *"All of you that are having a hard time believing that Jesus is here personally, come up here and stand where He's standing."* About 40 people came to the front to go to where Jesus was standing. When they got there, all collapsed under His power onto the floor. It was powerful! All skeptics hit the floor under the power of God for Jesus had touched them all without using me. I was still sitting down on the steps, just watching all of this and thinking about how powerful and how delightful it was! There's nothing like watching Jesus minister! I love Him working with us!

Jesus Appears in Denny's

One day, during my special prayer time before a crusade, I heard the Lord say to me, *"Go to Denny's restaurant, for I'm going to appear to you there."* I replied back to the Lord, *"Is this really you?"* I asked because I would usually stay inside and pray the night before a crusade. Then He replied back, *"Yes. Go because I have an appointment with you there."* So I gathered two of my pastors and we went to Denny's. I told them what the Lord said to me: that He was going to walk into Denny's and meet us there. They had always seen the Lord keep His promise in showing up in the Crusades.

When we arrived I didn't know what to do but sit there and wait. There were people there in the restaurant and we waited.

Many Slain Under the Power in Denny's

About 30 to 40 minutes went by and then I suddenly saw the Lord walk into the restaurant! All of a sudden, the atmosphere in Denny's was filled with glory and electricity. We could feel it, and the people could feel it—even the sinners. Then, without us doing anything, the waiter and other people started gathering to our table asking us about what they were feeling in the room. We began witnessing to them about the Lord and prayed for them. Before it was all over, a growth disappeared off a young man and unbelievers were delivered that are still saved to this very day! Many people in that restaurant were slain under the power of God on the floor. It was glorious. I didn't know He was going to do this. I learned that it's just better to obey God's voice even if you don't understand it. I thought in my mind...Denny's? Why? But it was glorious!

Cancers Healed Through Jesus' Appearance in Detroit

The most amazing thing happened to me during this season. In 2004, I was scheduled to be at a church that a friend of mine, Wayne T. Jackson, was pastoring. At this time we had just met, so we didn't know each other very well. Before I flew out to his church in Detroit on Saturday, I was invited to a Pastor Benny Hinn crusade from Thursday through Friday. I've always liked going to Pastor Benny Hinn's crusades. The presence of the Lord is so thick and glorious there. As I was in Pastor Benny's Friday morning miracle service, Jesus appeared to me during the beautiful atmosphere of worship. He walked up to me in the physical realm. He then began talking to me saying, *"I'm sending you to this pastor's church for a special purpose, and to bring a release and breakthrough to his personal life, destiny, and ministry. This will be the sign unto him that I have sent you. He has two members in his church, Tiffany and Karen. These two have dormant tumors in their bodies that will spread all over their body, killing them in a short period of time. I am going to heal them. Mention this to him and he will know that I have sent you.*" Bishop Jackson and I had only spoken on the phone at this point and had never met in person.

After this, Jesus walked away and disappeared. When I flew in on Saturday, I sat down with him in his beautiful mansion and shared with him everything Jesus told me about his members. He gave witness to this saying that he did have two members by those names. He knew Karen had tumors, but he didn't know Tiffany also had them. I told him that on Sunday I would openly share with the church what the Lord said to me and call for Karen and Tiffany to come up to the front. So I did, and Karen came forth, but Tiffany wasn't there that day. I told Karen what the Lord said, and then I prayed for her. That day she passed two to three tumors out of her body. I found out later that Karen had 30 pounds of tumors in her body and had not been working because of their debilitating effect on her body.

These tumors left her unable to work for three to four months. Over the next two to three months she passed the remaining pounds of tumors out of her body. Jesus is so powerful! In this same move we saw the Lord do a lot of glorious things. Jesus then appeared to me again in this Bishop's mansion. He walked straight through the wall and said, "*I've sent you here because my servant has been losing momentum and I've come to give you an assessment of what he needs to do for his church to catch up, flourish, and gain the momentum that it once had. Because he has a "power" ministry, he has been hindered by a spirit of tradition and religion that is in the building.*"

Jesus went on to tell me that his church attendance took a dive because there was a spirit of religion in the building he was renting. The people that owned the building had a religious spirit, and religion hinders the power of God from flowing. This bishop has a "power" ministry from God in which supernatural miracles are evident in his life. This man of God received this word and obeyed the Lord's instruction and his church began to instantly and supernaturally flourish.

A Dominican Pastor Encounters Jesus and His Church Breaks Into Revival

I met a Dominican pastor who came to the United States to experience a move of God in one of our cities. His life was dramatically changed! We saw God do miraculous things including healings and salvations. It was wonderful! The Lord started visiting scores of pastors and many of our youth in face-to-face appearances. When this Dominican pastor heard this, He cried to the Lord saying, *"Lord, I want to see you. I need this face-to-face relationship with you."* Nothing happened on his three-day visit to America. So, when he went back home he believed that the Lord would do this in his life and ministry. He went to sleep on a Tuesday and he suddenly saw Jesus in a white robe talking to Him in a dream saying, *"I will return to you and meet you at the church on Sunday...."* After this he woke up! That following Sunday, after this appearance from the Lord, Jesus did as he said and visited the service and a revival broke out at this pastor's church. As a result they started having revival in the Dominican Republic. How Awesome! This face-to-face relationship with the Lord will serve as the key for true revival for you wonderful and faithful pastors that have been waiting for a move of God to break out in your church, city, and country.

Jesus Appears and Physically Walks at Miracle Service in Jacksonville, Florida

I was invited to Jacksonville, Florida, to visit a church that is pastored by R.J. Washington who is a great man of God. He is a great friend of ours even to this day! Pastor Washington asked me

MY TRIP TO HEAVEN

to come to his church to do a set of miracle services. We had an awesome time in these services. On one of these nights, I told the people, as I always did, how Jesus promised me that He would make a special trip from Heaven to earth to be with us in the service. I told them that He allows me to conduct the meeting, but when He comes He promises to heal the sick. On this night Jesus visibly appeared to me and walked through the audience. Again my eyes were opened to see Him, and I narrated His movements as I had done before in other services. The service was already awesome and miracles were taking place, but then He came to make it even better!

As I saw Him in this service, I told the people where He was. Now you have to understand that this was a big auditorium, so it would be easy to miss where I was pointing because I was standing on the platform and He was moving around the huge floor. I described His movements toward a section on the right side of the auditorium and I pointed specifically to where He was standing. He looked up at me and said, *"I'm touching a young man named Richard right here in this section where I'm standing."* I told the people that Jesus was touching a young man named Richard in this section. A young man started jumping up and down saying "That's me! That's me! Here I am!"

Richard was standing where Jesus was standing. I wasn't operating out of the prophetic or words of knowledge, I was just sharing the intimacy of Jesus being in the room with everyone. The atmosphere in the room was filled with ecstatic electricity, and the crowd was filled with great faith. This was the highlight of the night, even though we saw great miracles, signs, and wonders take place in that service. The people knew I wasn't imagining things. They saw that I accurately talked about Jesus' movements in the room and Richard's testimony was the proof.

Jesus Appears in the City of Chicago in 2007

We also saw this happen in Chicago where one of the greatest visible manifestations of God's glory, the face of Jesus Christ, was revealed. One of my sons in ministry pastors in Chicago and he came to me one day saying, *"I had a dream about you coming to Chicago, and when you came a move of God broke out and people came from everywhere."* I didn't know how long it would take this dream to come to pass, because when God shows dreams there is often an interval before they are fulfilled. So I held this dream he had in respect and waited for it to come to pass. In April 2006, I was seeking the Lord in Port Huron at the church of Dad and Mother Nichols who are Juanita Bynum's spiritual parents. Jesus appeared in the room in front of me saying, *"I am about to fulfill the covenant that I made with you in the year 2001. Now my Father will join me in working with you in notable ways in front of My Church body and the world."* He then went on to tell me that thousands, even millions, in America were about to experience open appearances from Him in dreams and in broad daylight! After Jesus told me this and some other things, I had no idea when this season would begin. Later that year it suddenly took place! A move of God hit Washington State and as a result Juanita Bynum's sister-in-law, Samantha Bynum, heard about it. She is a pastor and prophetess in Chicago and has such a hunger for God. When she heard about the Lord appearing in Seattle and Washington State, she asked if I could come to Chicago to her church and wondered if the Lord could do something like this in Chicago. I replied, *"Sure."* I then said, *"Before long, the Lord is going to allow every state in America to experience a visitation from Him like this."* So she asked me to come because of these things. The Lord told me to go, so I did. We scheduled one week of services from Monday through Friday. We had an awesome time, but something unusual took place.

A Move of God Hit Chicago

While I was preaching on the third night of the service, Jesus appeared in the middle of the service in the aisle in front of me. I mean He literally interrupted me as I was preaching at the height and climax of my message. When I saw Him, I abruptly stopped preaching and gazed at Him. Jesus stood there so regally and awesome like He has at other times when I have seen Him. He had on the beautiful, cleaner-than-white robe that I have usually seen Him in. He started to speak to me saying, *"David, I am about to walk the streets of Chicago and prepare this city for a move of God and at the appointed time I will bring you back here."* Now you have to understand that the people saw me stop preaching and start gazing for a minute. They wondered what was happening and why I stopped preaching abruptly at the height of my message. They did not see Jesus, but I did. The Lord disappeared; He left just as suddenly as He came. I then told the audience and pastor what had just happened. They rejoiced and believed God. I finished up the next two nights and finally went home to rest. The day after these services, Pastor Bynum was on the streets of Chicago taking care of some business when she ran into a woman whom she didn't know. The lady came up to her saying she felt led to show her some pictures and that she hadn't shown these pictures to anyone else.

When she showed Prophetess Bynum these pictures, she was astonished because the pictures showed Jesus walking the streets of Chicago. The lady began sharing with her that she had been on the street of Chicago taking pictures of the buildings, and all the pictures came out normal except four of them that were unusual. In two out of these four pictures, you can plainly see Jesus walking the streets of Chicago with one foot up off the ground. I put the pictures in this book to prove that Jesus is still alive and that He is making notable appearances in America! Pastor Bynum was astonished when she saw these pictures saying, *"The Lord is doing what He promised! He appeared to an apostle in my church a few days ago and said He was going to walk the streets of Chicago and He has."* Samantha Bynum got copies and brought them to show me. When I saw them, I was astonished and encouraged at the same time!

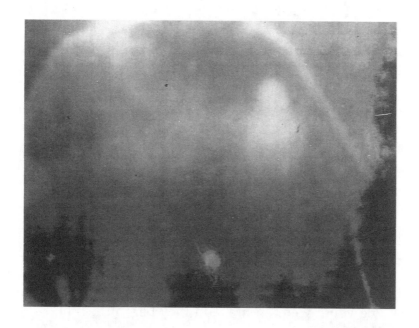

The following year, 2007, a move of God hit Chicago. Thousands of people traveled from five different continents of the world and 25 different states in America to experience it. It was awesome! Night after night salvations and miracles took place. It was tremendous! The youth were on fire, and they began catching on when about 250 of them started having face-to-face visitations from the Lord. It was amazing! Jesus had prepared Chicago for a move of God, and it was taking place! It's an experience I'll never forget! The Lord is going to visit America in this way on a broader scale! This is an exciting time for America and the nations of the earth.

Chapter 6

My Special Trip to
Heaven in the Year 2000

"Jesus Walks Me Around Heaven"

SOMETHING UNEXPECTED HAPPENED to me in the year 2000, and it turned out to be one of the greatest experiences I've ever had. Almost suddenly and without warning I was taken to Heaven again while sleeping. This time I wasn't taken to Heaven for just a few seconds or minutes to hear a message from Jesus and then returned to earth. In this visitation I got a chance to stay a little longer with Jesus. He walked me around and presented me to saints who had served the Lord in power when they had lived on earth, and I was able to get answers to many of the questions I had at the time. This visitation appearance from the Lord is one I will cherish for the rest of my life. By this time it was already established that I loved the Lord with all my heart and that He alone was my focus. I've heard different ones say that when they first get to Heaven they want to see their deceased mother, father, or someone else dear to them. Not so with me! Jesus is the first person that I desire to see once I cross over into eternity.

Immediately, I was standing in the spirit in front of Jesus. He looked so joyful, and He had a pleasant smile on His face. When

I first saw Him, He didn't say anything to me. He just took me around to talk with different people who had once lived on earth. I was familiar with some of them, because I had studied their lives. We approached two men. The first man was tall and slender, and I knew in my spirit that he had been an evangelist when he lived on earth, but I didn't recognize him. I did recognize the second man because I had studied his life; it was Smith Wigglesworth!

Smith Wigglesworth ministered in the early 1900s and God used him to raise 23 people from the dead! He also had a powerful miracle and healing ministry! Jesus stood beside me but said nothing as if He wanted these great servants of His to tell me what I was about to hear. You see, I didn't realize it at the time, but Jesus brought me to Heaven to hear and understand some important things that would serve as the foundation, catalyst, and confirmation of my whole life and ministry. As Jesus and I stood side-by-side facing these two men, the evangelist began talking. I also noticed that he was taller than both Jesus and I. Jesus stands a little taller than I do. I'm about 5 feet 8 inches tall and Jesus has always been a tad bit taller than me in every visitation I've had. The evangelist started telling me that I had lost a lot of the power that God had given me in that season as a result of my lack of consecration. He also went on to tell me that this had also caused the attendance and crowds to drop in my meetings.

I stood there and listened to this because all those things were true. I had noticed that the crowds and overall attendance had decreased in our meetings. I had failed to pay the price in this season for the anointing and power of God! I had missed the mark. You see, when we as preachers slack up in our consecrated walk with God, these areas in our ministry are affected. After this trip to Heaven, I studied the lives of great men and women and learned that when they failed to consecrate themselves they lost power, the attendance in their meetings decreased, their families were lost to them, and some even lost their own lives. The anointing that we operate out of is hindered. The gravitational pull from God's presence on our life and ministry that attracts large crowds will also diminish. We must pay the price of death to self by living a consecrated life. As you read on, I will share how God gives us all grace and power to move on to victory even after we fail horribly.

I Talked With Smith Wigglesworth in Heaven

Before I could think about what the evangelist said to me, Smith Wigglesworth interjected and gave me a divine answer regarding how to come back from where I had fallen short and how to regain momentum. He said, *"David, go back and study the great men and women that God used in a significant way."* I didn't realize it at the time, but this statement opened up a glorious revelation that Jesus began illuminating to me. I wrote about this experience in another book for sake of time. I had already studied some of Smith Wigglesworth's life, and I knew that he didn't read any books besides the Bible, nor did He allow any other publications in his house like magazines, newspapers, or even other books written by Christian authors.

This sounded a little overboard to me, but now I was in Heaven and Wigglesworth had changed. He was telling me to go study the history of great men and women of God stretching back to the time of Abraham and Moses. I had much more studying to do! The neat thing was to see the change in him. He was now counseling me to go study other books about those who lived in our day as well as those who lived in biblical times. I also noticed that Hebrew's description of Heaven is accurate:

> But ye are come unto mount Sion, and unto the city of
> the living God, the heavenly Jerusalem, and to an innu-
> merable company of angels, To the general assembly, and
> church of the firstborn, which are written in heaven, and

to God the Judge of all, and to the spirits of just men made perfect (Hebrews 12:22-23).

He is now operating in total perfection. I saw this just in the fact that he encouraged me to read biographical accounts of other men and women of God. Smith also looked a little bit thinner in Heaven than he did in the pictures I had seen of him.

I Walked and Talked With Kathryn Kuhlman in Heaven and She's Still a Redhead

Another person I saw in glory was Kathryn Kuhlman. I have always wondered about how she was able to attract God's presence to her life like she did. I had read stories about how the glory of God was so powerful on her life. On one occasion, she walked through the back of a Holiday Inn Hotel at the end of a service to avoid the crowds. The presence of the Holy Spirit attended her so strongly. When she passed through the kitchen, all the staff had their backs turned to her and didn't realize who she was or that she was even walking through their kitchen. As she passed by them, they began to collapse on the floor under the power of God. Their hats, spoons, aprons, and everything fell on the floor with them as they were slain by the mighty power of God that attended Kathryn. She hadn't stopped to pray for or even touch them! I always thought that was amazing! I also heard a story about a special service Kathryn ministered in. God sent heavenly electricity that physically manifested to an audience of 12,000 to 20,000 people with spectacular miracles following. Now that's power! Another service Kathryn was ministering in experienced a strong, tornado-like wind that started blowing in her service. Multiple miracles began taking place that astounded people!

These testimonies have always intrigued me, and I have always wondered how she got God's presence on her life like that! Well,

I had the chance to ask her about this while we were standing in Heaven. As I stood there, I looked at this tall woman evangelist. She looked so glorious, and she had on a white dress with ruffles in it. I also noticed that her hair was red. She also looked much younger in Heaven compared to the pictures I saw of her around the age of their death. You see, God will renew our youth in Heaven! You too can have an experience like this—a trip to Heaven—if you would but ask the Lord for it!

When I initially saw Kathryn, I had to run to catch up with her because she was walking over a beautiful, golden bridge in the opposite direction of where Jesus and I were. It had a small stream of crystal clear water flowing under it. I still remember this moment even today. This stream of water was so beautiful, clear, and pure. It was on this golden bridge that I caught up to her and asked the question that I always wanted to know concerning God's presence in her life and ministry. When I saw her, she was already moving, but I soon quickly caught up with her. I asked her, *"Kathryn, how did you get the Lord on your life like this?"* She replied with fire-filled eyes and a very serious look on her face, *"Don't stop preaching the word of God and, furthermore, don't desecrate!"* After she said these words, she walked away. She was giving me a valuable lesson. I understood what she meant by the first statement, to never stop preaching the word of God, but I had never heard the word desecrate nor knew what it meant.

There it was. I had my answer. Later, when I arrived back at home from this spiritual trip to Heaven, I looked up the word desecrate. To desecrate means "To violate or to treat with irreverence." It also means "To disrespect holy things or dead things."[1] I know that Kathryn taught a lot about death to self and paying the price, which is achieved by dying a spiritual death to our desires and will. What I understood her to say to me was that the price for what she walked in required that she preach the word, because God confirms his word with signs and wonders.

The second point she was making is that once you die to self, you should not desecrate your death. Usually the word desecrate is used in association with someone going to a burial site and being irreverent to the dead in some way. She was saying that once you pay the price to die (because at this point in my walk I had) don't go back and dig yourself up; don't mourn your death. Stay dead to self! Don't allow self to resurrect and desecrate the sacred holy life you now walk as a Christian. She was essentially telling me not to become spiritually defiled or unclean. That's the price, death to self, but stay dead after you die to self. Don't go back and mess with your burial. We do this by reverting back to the flesh! May God help us all to not do this!

Bishop C.H. Mason Gives Me a Message

Bishop Mason Is Still Dancing in Heaven

I was allowed to fellowship with and see another great man of God on this trip to Heaven. He was used powerfully at the turn of the century and was inspired by the Azusa Street Revival. His name was Bishop C.H. Mason. Through his encounter and baptism of the Holy Spirit, Mason founded the Church of God in Christ (COGIC), which is currently the largest Pentecostal denomination in the United States. I grew up in a COGIC church and have been so blessed by the things I learned from my Bishop G.E. Patterson in his lifetime from this movement. When Bishop Mason first began this denomination, it had a very strong move of God upon it. This mighty apostle was known to walk in the building among thousands of people, and tumors and growths would instantly fall on the floor. He had a powerful healing and miracle ministry. I grew up in Memphis, Tennessee, where his headquarters were and I heard from those who knew him concerning the powerful services he conducted. The glory of God also attended this man in an unusual way.

As I approached him, he told me that this mighty denomination and movement had lost the glory it once had. The Lord also told me that He is going to restore the glory of God back to the Church of God in Christ as it once was but in an even greater way! He began telling me that when has was alive on earth, the Holy Spirit would come upon him and he would just start breaking out in a dance before the Lord and the music had to catch up with him. Like a loving spiritual father, he said, *"David, now many of my children [COGIC] dance to the music instead of dancing according to the Holy Spirit."* He explained, *"They wait on the music to get started instead of being led by the Spirit of God."* He told me to tell them to go back to dancing in the Spirit. Then suddenly, he started dancing to show me how he danced before the Lord while on earth. It was powerful! Glory filled the place in Heaven where we were. I saw that miracles took place when he danced on earth. After this visitation, I saw an old tape of Bishop Mason dancing, and he was dancing in the same way I had seen him dance in Heaven. Wow! This was a tremendous experience!

Jesus Encourages Me in Heaven

Appearances in Glory

Jesus is so humble. I was so amazed at His humility. He is the King of kings, but He stood there silently allowing His servants to minister and talk to me. You would think that you would only talk to Jesus or the angels when you're in Heaven. It never occurred to me that He would allow His own servants to talk to me while He was standing there. Some think that it is bizarre that the Lord would allow saints to give us messages, but this is not unscriptural and was not unheard of in Jesus' day. The Father allowed Moses and Elijah to appear to Jesus in glory to talk to Him about accomplishing His earthly ministry concerning dying on the cross.

Why the Lord Allows Saints That Have Passed on to Talk to Us

After my trip to Heaven, one of the things that Smith Wigglesworth said was revealed to me in Scripture. Wigglesworth told me to go search and study the lives of spiritual Fathers tracing all the way back to the past.

> *For ask now of the days that are past, which were before thee, since the day that God created man upon the earth,* and ask from the one side of heaven unto the other *(Deuteronomy 4:32).*

> *For enquire, I pray thee, of the former age, and prepare thyself to the search of their fathers.* (For we are but of yesterday, and know nothing, because our days upon earth are a shadow:) Shall not they teach thee, and tell thee, and utter words out of their heart? (Job 8:8-10)

The Bible says that we need to ask or inquire about the past days. This passage in Deuteronomy also says that our asking should not just be on this side of life but that it should extend to Heaven. Wow! Why? The second Scripture tells us that we are at a disadvantage because we have not lived long and our time here is limited. The Scripture is telling us that we will learn more if we ask for wisdom from those who have gone before us.

God's Purpose for Allowing This to Happen in Our Lives

The Lord allowed these men and women to answer questions about my destiny (and other things) that I needed to know to be successful in my personal call and ministry. Elijah and Moses came to speak to Jesus for the same reason. After preaching the message that Smith Wigglesworth gave me, there was such glory released that a woman was raised from the dead in the middle of the service!

This served to confirm this message and was a sign that Smith Wigglesworth's anointing somehow transferred to me while we talked. I could share much more with you about this visit to Heaven, but for sake of time I cannot write everything in this book. You can hear the entire story of my trip to Heaven on CD or DVD.

The conversations I had with these godly men and women were filled with advice, wisdom, and instruction on how to finish my assignment on Earth successfully. The Bible calls these type of experiences *Appearances in Glory* (in The Glory Realm or Heavenly Realm).

> *And, behold, there talked with him two men, which were Moses and Elias: Who **appeared in glory,** and spake of his decease which he should accomplish at Jerusalem* (Luke 9:30-31).

Jesus brought up saints from the grave when He rose from the dead. He made a stop on earth with the saints, who had been held captive in hell, before continuing on to Heaven for the first time. During this stop on earth, the Bible records that many of the saints who once lived, like David and Jeremiah, appeared to many people in the Holy City.

> *And the graves were opened; and many bodies of saints which slept arose' And came out of the graves after his resurrection, and went into the holy city, and appeared unto many* (Matthew 27: 52-53).

Prominence in Heaven: They Knew Who I Was in Heaven

> *Whosoever therefore shall confess me before men, him will I confess also before my Father which is in heaven; But whosoever shall deny me before men, him*

will I also deny before my Father which is in heaven (Matthew 10:32-33).

*Also I say unto you, **whosoever shall confess me before men, him shall the Son of man also confess before the angels of God**; But he that denieth me before men shall be denied before the angels of God* (Luke 12:8-9).

Whosoever therefore shall be ashamed of me and of my words in this adulterous and sinful generation; of him also shall the Son of man be ashamed, *when he cometh in the glory of his Father with the holy angels* (Mark 8:38).

As I passed by the saints and angels, everyone seemed to already know me. I then asked the Lord, *"How do they know me? I've never met them nor all the angels that seemed to stand at attention around me."* Then Jesus answered me saying, *"David, everyone here knows you because I have spoken of you to them."* He went on saying, *"Do you remember in My Word where I said if you confess Me before men, I will confess you to My Father and My holy angels, but if you deny Me before men on earth, I will deny you saying 'I don't know you'?"*

He continued, *"You have been a bold witness before men on earth, telling them of your passionate love for Me, and I have done the same for you here. You have not been ashamed of Me or My words before the world. I have confessed your name and person to My Father here in Heaven; He knows you because of Me. These angels know of you because I told them you were with Me."*

The Lord Wants to Spread Your Name Around Heaven Too

Then I remembered all the times I had witnessed to people about Jesus since I was 17. I remember spending quality time with the homeless, sometimes 12 to 20 hours or even sleeping all night on the street, just to lead as many people to the Lord as I could. We saw thousands saved over the years through this! I was so happy to know that Jesus took notice of this. You too, as you witness and confess Jesus before men in this world, will cause your name to be spread like fame throughout Heaven from the lips of Jesus Himself. You may ask, *"What things does He say about me in Heaven?"* He speaks the testimony of the spiritual life you established with Him. He also confesses your name to His Father.

> *He that overcometh...I will confess his name before My Father, and before His angels* (Revelation 3:5).

> *And the Lord said unto Moses, I will do this thing also that thou hast spoken: For thou hast found grace in My sight, and I know thee by name* (Exodus 33:17; see also Exodus 33:12).

What an honor and privilege it is to be spoken of highly and prominently by the King of kings and Lord of lords. Jesus then replied, *"When you talk about Me on earth David, I talk about you in Heaven and on earth. I speak well of you to others and have appeared to your enemies who have persecuted you. I confess you, because in your love for Me you have confessed Me. I love you and will also confess you more. This is just the beginning."* He continued, *"Now let Me introduce you to the most important relationship and person in My life, My Father. He's been waiting on you, for I have already spoken of you to Him."*

I Saw the Beautiful City of God: Mount Zion

When I was in Heaven I briefly caught a glimpse of Mount Zion, the city of God. As I saw this beautiful city, I noticed that its landscape was on a slope and was a fair-sized mound or hill but not necessarily an extremely high mountain as some would think.

I recognized this because as I was approaching the city with thousands of others, we were walking upward toward the highest point where the Father was sitting. At one point, I remember looking at those around me and recognized that we all had on beautiful, white robes. We were all marching and moving toward the city, and I was happy to be among those who I knew were redeemed. We walked up steps toward the city where the bright light of the Lord was shining from the top of the hill. Thousands of saints were there.

Later I discovered that these thousands of saints are what the Bible calls the general assembly or the mass gathering of the people of God. I saw the beautiful, golden walls that surrounded the city. Heaven is a real place, and it has been prepared for you, your children, your family, and all your loved ones. The Lord also let me climb one of these golden walls—they were so beautiful and made of translucent gold that I could see through them.

Our Lives Are Written in Heavenly Books

Your Assignment and Destiny Is Already Written

Thou tellest my wanderings...are they not in thy book? (Psalm 56:8)

Then said I, Lo, I come: in the volume of the book it is written of me (Psalm 40:7).

I Saw Our Books in Heaven

I had another experience early in my walk that I think is important to share with you. In 1992, I was 19 years old, and I was given the opportunity to see another room in Heaven. I was single at the time and had planned to marry a commendable, Christian woman, so I asked the Lord if marrying her was His will for my life. That night when I fell asleep I was taken to Heaven in a dream. Immediately, I was sucked out of my body and was taken to Heaven at the speed of thought. I was just there! When I arrived, I was only permitted to go inside one room that was filled with huge books that had everyone's life written down inside. I knew that these were the books written by God, and they contained His plans and purposes for everyone who had ever been born or who would be born. These books were the size of those giant, family-sized, coffee table Bibles, and they were white and gold.

The hilarious thing about this visitation is that I became curious about everyone else's books, so I ran over to take a look at them, but an angel beckoned me to come away and look at my book. This angel was about seven to eight feet tall, and he had on a white robe.

In the center of this round room were shelves filled with these white and gold books. The room looked like a humongous library with shelves around the wall, and in the center of the room stood a podium with my personal white and gold book on it. The angel was standing next to it beckoning me to come close. When I walked up to the podium, the book that the Lord had written about my whole life was already opened. At the top left side of this book was written, "**GOD'S PLAN**," and everything I was ordained to do by God at the age of nineteen was written underneath it. This book didn't look like a book from earth, because it was blank on the right side. I understood that God left this blank side for me to fill as I made choices during my life. As I made them, these choices would be written down alongside the life He had ordained for me before the foundation of the world.

All of a sudden words appeared in bold letters on the right side of the book that said, "**DAVID'S BIGGEST DIVORCEMENT**." Then the angel plainly answered my prayer regarding whether I should marry this woman or not: "*The Lord says your life will be a disaster if you marry her, and you'll mess up the special ministry in your* *life."* After this, I woke up out of the dream. I didn't even know I was called to have a special ministry! I was only nineteen years old, and I had just gotten saved two years earlier. Most people don't know that God has written down our lives in books. These books include His plans and purposes for us, and even whom we should or should not marry! The Lord used this dream to communicate this to me. Look at this Scripture:

> *Then said I, Lo, I come (in the volume of the book it is written of me) to do thy will, oh God* (Hebrews 10:7).

The writer of Hebrews is saying that there was a book that contained the will of God for Jesus' life in it. We each also have a book and I have seen mine! Also, David mentions in Psalms that God wrote his life down in a book.

> *Let them be blotted out of the book of the living, and not be written with the righteous* (Psalm 69:28).

> *Thine eyes did see my substance, yet being unperfect; and in thy book all my members were written, which in continuance were fashioned; when as yet there was none of them* (Psalm 139:16).

> *Thou tellest my wanderings…are they not in thy book?* (Psalm 56:8)

Here again in these passages of Scripture we see the Holy Spirit speaking through David that the Lord has recorded our lives in books. This dream was pivotal to the success of my life and destiny. I was about to marry the wrong person and it could have destroyed the plans God had for my life. God used this dream to preserve my destiny! How many people do you know that have married the wrong person? Their whole life may have ended in shambles, but they might have avoided a lifetime of heartache and pain if they had just a dream like this. Even if you have experienced the disaster of marrying the wrong person or going through a divorce, there is still hope through the Lord's mercy to turn these negative circumstances around. Nothing is impossible with God, and He can still give you a bright future and make something beautiful out of your life!

Jesus Reveals the Great Mystery: Christ in Us, the Hope of Glory

After this Jesus took me to see a great truth and mystery in Heaven. By this time in 2000 I had seen Jesus walk in my services and crusades on the earth. When I told people about it, some believed me, but many others did not. Jesus then spoke to me saying, *"David, I've come to reveal two great mysteries to you and to My church."* At this point, a screen appeared that displayed one of the services I had conducted that was part of a crusade. Jesus stood beside me and prompted me to watch. As I watched the service, I saw myself on the stage pacing back and forth with the microphone in my hand and preaching the gospel boldly. Suddenly, Jesus prompted me to look closely so I could see a great mystery. I watched myself walk off the stage and down the platform.

As I walked off the stage, I looked back on the stage, and Jesus had a microphone in his hand and was preaching the gospel. He was wearing a white robe. It's like I walked outside of Him. Then Jesus said to me, *"I've come to tell you and My church the mystery of Christ in you—the hope of Glory for the world."* Then He said to me, *"When you ask me to come take over your body and mouth, David, I do this before you minister."* He said another truth, *"I dwell inside of you; I walk in you."* He said, *"The moment you start ministering and you feel like you want to start pacing the floor, walking, and ministering...that's not you, it's Me! Did I not promise that I will walk in you and dwell in you. Tell My people that I walk in them and dwell inside of their physical bodies; for your bodies are My temple."* Wow! I had always sensed the Lord's presence with me in services, and at times in a special way, but not all the time. But here He was showing me that He was entering in and out of my body while ministering to the saints. I often didn't feel anything special or unusual happening even though I saw spectacular miracles take place during the services.

I didn't know this was happening to me like Moses didn't know when the glory of God was upon his face! Or like when Jacob said God's presence was with him. He said, *"Surely the Lord is in this place; and I knew it not"* (Gen. 28:16). This is what happened to me. I didn't know that this was really happening while I was ministering. I knew Jesus was showing me this because the Scripture says ***"Know ye not your ownselves, how that Jesus Christ is in you..."*** (2 Cor. 13:5). He was also revealing the truth in this Scripture:

> *To whom God would **make known** what is the riches of the glory of this mystery among the Gentiles, which is **Christ in you, the hope of glory*** (Colossians 1:27).

> *...for ye are the temple of the Living God; as **God hath said, I will dwell in them, and walk in them; and I will be their God and they shall be My people*** (2 Corinthians 6:16).

Jesus Personally Appears and Heals the Sick in Crusades

He then had me turn to finish watching. I watched myself walk back onto the stage and into Jesus and I was speaking again. I knew I had walked back inside of Jesus. Then the Lord said, *"You've also asked Me to work with you personally in ministry and I've brought you here to show you that I do. You may have lost a lot of the anointing I've given you in this season of your life, but I've given you something greater to replace that. I've given you Me, and My own personal Glory. I will now come and work with you in every service at the moment you stand on the stage."* Something glorious happened after I walked back inside of Jesus. He said, *"Behold! Watch!"* I again saw Jesus walk out of my physical body and off the stage but this time He kept walking. When I saw Him walk out there among the people, I followed Him off the stage and He started touching and healing sick people and those in wheelchairs. There were people in this service that had been in wheelchairs for years, and Jesus touched them so slightly that they didn't realize they were healed.

Then He said to me, *"You must get off the stage and co-labor with Me by helping them out of their wheelchairs and showing them that I've accomplished healing in their bodies."* I felt so honored that the King of kings would personally work with me. Then Jesus said to me, *"I also brought you here to build up and encourage confidence, in you and in My people. Tell them that I will personally make trips to earth during the miracle crusades I give you to conduct. Let them know I will meet with them in a special way when they come, that I will heal their sick."* It was amazing! I knew that the Lord was working with me when He started to appear to those I witnessed to in 1996, but this was even more encouraging! This encounter gave me the boldness to share what He was telling me with the audience, and since this encounter in 2000, we have seen Him do miracles, healings, and meet with the masses in every miracle crusade!

Passing the Twenty-four Elders

After this, Jesus and I walked toward the Father's throne and passed by the twenty-four elders that sit around it. I had always wanted to know why the Lord had twenty-four elders around His throne (see Rev. 4:4). I knew that elders were spiritual advisors.

When I studied this passage, I wondered why the Lord would need spiritual advisors around His throne since He is God and knows everything. After all, who can instruct or advise Him? When I asked Jesus about this, He said to me:

> *These elders do not give Me advice of themselves. They are the determinate counsel. Remember, David, I live My own word and it says that purposes are established in the multitude of counselors.*

> *Without counsel purposes are disappointed: but in the multitude of counselors they are established* (Proverbs 15:22).

> *I wouldn't tell you to live what I don't first live Myself. These counselors are not here for the same reason that an earthly counselor would be called upon. They cannot counsel My Father or Me about anything from within themselves, but they advise us concerning My word and what We have already said. Remember it says:*

> *Put me in remembrance...* (Isaiah 43:26).

> *They can only speak to My Father that which has already been spoken. My Father places His Word above His name. Just because His name is Almighty Jehovah doesn't mean He's free to not abide by His own word. He is bound and committed to His word to perform it. My death on the cross was by the foreknowledge of My Father and this determinate counsel. The plan of salvation was determined before the world began by My Father. Decisions and discussions are made in Heaven, ages before earthly time began, David."*

> *Him, being delivered by the determinate counsel and foreknowledge of God,* ye have taken, and by wicked hands have crucified and slain *(Acts 2:23).*

These men were glorious. I understood the Lord to mean that these men were like an executive board of counsel, but they operate differently in the Heavenly realm than in the earthly realm. These men cannot advise God in their own strength or wisdom. They must solely consult with Him and determine things according to His word, because the Lord has placed His word above His name. He honors His word highly! Wow! God submits and commits to obey His own word. What integrity!

Jesus Allows Me to Come to the Throne Room of the Father

"I Saw the Father's Glory in Heaven"

Jesus Shows Me the Father

I also got to experience being before the Father's throne in Heaven. Immediately, I was taken into a huge room and there was Glory all around. The power in that place was so overwhelming that I could not stand up on my feet. I was quickly on my face before I knew what was happening to me! The light was so brilliant that I could not see clearly. While my face was flat on the floor, I could lift myself up just enough to see how the floor looked. It was beautiful marble stone with veins running through it. It was then that I realized I was lying prostrate on a floor of marble. I then lifted my head up a little higher, and I saw Father God sitting on a huge throne. I was lying about 5 to 10 feet away prostrated before His feet. The light, glory, and clouds were so bright that I could not look up high enough to see His face. My spiritual body also retained no strength in it. I was completely weak in His presence.

All I could do was barely lift my head. When I looked up again, I saw Him plainly sitting on his throne with His arms and hands resting on the throne's armrests. He was wearing a beautiful, gold wedding band on His gentle finger. Out of this whole experience of being in front of the Father's throne, it was this ring that stood out to me most! I wondered why the Father wears a wedding band on His finger. The Lord God didn't say anything verbally to me. I didn't have the strength to lift myself up high enough to see His face. It was awesome, and I know that like many others you will also have a trip like this to Heaven before you die.

Jesus Explains the Wedding Ring on the Father's Hand

Afterwards, Jesus began to explain the significance of the wedding band that I saw the Father wearing. He said, *"David, My Father and I are betrothed in marriage to you. He that is joined unto the Lord is one spirit with Him in marriage."* Then He said, *"You have reached the betrothal stage in marriage with God!"* Then He went on to explain saying:

There's a difference in My kingdom with those who love me." He said, *"Everyone who is a believer is not necessarily part of the elect or married to Me in this level of union."* Then He said further, *"There is a difference in relationship levels with Me. I will be as close and intimate as you will allow Me to be. Like in the natural realm, there is a difference between friendship, sonship, servanthood, stewardship, kingship, and the marriage relationship. You are more obligated to your spouse than you are to your friends. You may love your friends, but you live, abide, and dwell with your spouse. The commitment you make to a marriage relationship is more intense and intimate than any other.*

Jesus continued: *"I am one with you. This was My prayer to the Father while I was on earth that you would be one with the Father and I. You are not the only one with Me in friendship, but you are also one with Us in a deeper sense by being joined unto the Father in betrothal. I am more dedicated and committed to My bride than My friends or to those who just believe in Me. You asked for this marriage level relationship, and the Father allowed you to see this so that you may know that you have entered into the Marriage Covenant with Us, not just friendship."*

When I got back to earth and researched, I found confirmation for this in Scripture in several places. When Paul was writing his first epistle to the Corinthians, the Holy Spirit had him admonish a certain group saying, *"But he that is **joined unto** the Lord is one spirit"* (1 Cor. 6:17). This word joined is also used in the context of marriage. Just a few verses before this, Paul also said, *"The body is for the Lord and the Lord for the body"* (1 Cor. 6:13). This verse helps explain why I saw Him walking in and out of my body. The Scripture also says, ***"As God hath said I will dwell in them and walk in them" (see 2 Cor. 6:16.)*** In marriage our body is also committed to our spouse. This is why the Spirit had Paul write these words about us being joined to the Lord before he started talking about natural marriage between a man and his wife (see 1 Cor. 7), because we should be married to the Lord first and foremost!

I also found other Scriptures that explain that the Father is betrothed in marriage to His chosen or elect.

> *And I will betroth thee unto me for ever; yea, I will betroth thee unto me in righteousness, and in judgment, and in lovingkindness, and in mercies. I will even betroth thee unto me in faithfulness: and thou shalt know the Lord* (Hosea 2:19-20).

> ***For thy Maker is thine husband;*** *the Lord of hosts is his name* (Isaiah 54:5).

Did you hear that? These Scriptures imply and plainly state that the Lord is our Husband and that He is betrothed to us forever in an everlasting covenant of marriage. Someone may say that these promises of a marriage covenant were only made with Israel, but this is not true! The Bible says that through Jesus' sacrifice and blood, we have been grafted into God's family and are reconciled to Him.

> *That at that time ye were without Christ, being aliens from the commonwealth of Israel, and **strangers from the covenants of promise,** having no hope, and without God in the world: **But now in Christ Jesus ye who sometimes were far off are made nigh by the blood of Christ** (Ephesians 2:12-13).*

When I saw this Scripture in Hosea, Jesus' words were explained to me. When He said to me, *"David, I am more committed to My bride by covenant than the regular believer."* In the Bible, the Lord's bride is also mentioned as the "elect lady."

> *The elder **unto the elect lady** and her children* (3 John 1:1).

Jesus also mentions elect believers:

> *And except those days should be shortened, there should no flesh be saved: but **for the elect's sake** those days shall be shortened* (Matthew 24:22).

Those who have dedicated themselves to the Lord in betrothal or marriage are in a more committed relationship with Him. This doesn't mean that those who give their lives to the Lord as believers are not saved or will not go to Heaven, but that those who have joined themselves to the Lord in this way have a greater commitment to Him, and God demonstrates a greater level of faithfulness toward them as well. That's what Hosea means when it says we are betrothed to Him in faithfulness, mercies, and judgment. When you are married to the Lord, He is more obligated to you, especially in keeping you saved, than to the normal believer. When you marry the Lord, He promises that He will be committed to us in faithfulness and in judgment.

In order to fulfill these promises, He will move and change the timing of things, because He loves us, especially if He sees our salvation or eternal security threatened by future circumstances. Jesus mentioned this when He said that no flesh would be saved during the *"great tribulation"* (see Matt. 24:21). Then He said, (listen to this carefully now!) but for My *"elect's sake those days will be shortened"* (see Matt. 24:22). His purpose for shortening the days and altering time was that the elect might be saved. Did you hear this? This means He will manipulate and control the time by shortening the days, because He has a covenant with His elect. Awesome! It's a privilege to be married to the Lord.

Another point to see is how He has committed to judge us as a part of our marriage covenant. This means He is especially obligated to judge us when there's something in our life that threatens our soul, salvation, or eternal life.

You may remember that He said in Hosea that He would betroth us to Him forever. This means that He is making an everlasting covenant with us. I don't believe in the lying doctrine that's going around that asserts that Christians are *"once saved, always saved."* I do believe though, that through this marriage covenant relationship with the Lord, we can enter into more protection and security to help ensure our salvation. We see an example of this when Paul spoke about delivering a sinner over to satan for the destruction of the flesh so that his spirit might be saved (see 1 Cor. 5:5). The Lord also admonishes us to judge ourselves or else He will.

For if we would judge ourselves, we should not be judged.
But when we are judged, we are chastened of the Lord, that

we should not be condemned with the world (1 Corinthians 11:31-32).

The Lord tells us that if we do not judge ourselves, He will judge us so that we will not be lost or condemned with the world. Wow, what a privilege! The Lord is so committed to us in this marriage covenant that He will judge and chasten us before He will let us be lost. After I read these two verses, the visitation I had in which the Lord delivered me over to satan and the one where He took me to hell to judge me both became clear to me. He was keeping His part of the covenant in marriage with me. You also don't have to stay at the believer stage. The Lord wants to marry you, but He will not force this on you. The Bible says, *"He that is joined to the Lord,"* meaning that you must be willing to be joined or committed to Him in this way (see 1 Cor. 6:17). It has been awesome to walk with Him in this way. I look back and realize that all the times He has judged me, it has been a manifestation of His marriage covenant with me. I was joined to Him in a special way!

Are You Married to the Lord Yet?

Now the question I want to ask you is whether you are married to the Lord or just a believer? You too can have this type of relationship with God if you are willing to marry the Lord. Just ask…just ask! Lift your hands right now and ask the Lord by saying, "Lord, I want to marry you."

At the time, I thought that this was one of the greatest experiences I could have had in the Father's throne room, but I didn't know that I would have an even greater experience a few years later that went way beyond this.

Jesus Walks Me Back to the Edge of Heaven and Waves Goodbye

"Jesus Personally Waves Goodbye to Me at Our Departure"

As Jesus walked me back to the edge of Heaven, neither one of us wanted to part ways. Jesus had a great smile on His face when He said these final words to me: *"Have intercessors pray for you."* As I walked away from Jesus to be taken back to the earth, He waved goodbye. After these last words, I was taken back to earth and was back in my body when I woke up. My body, my room, and everything around me were filled with electricity, power, and Glory! I was so blessed!

Jesus showed me that our face-to-face relationship would more than make up for what I had failed to do in paying the price. He decided to more than make up for my lack and stepped in to work with me personally on earth in these services. That's what a real friend does, you know? They step in for you when you fail, and they cover you. The personal anointing on my life had decreased in services, but His glory in my life and ministry as a result of Him coming personally in the services went to an astronomical level which more than made up for this loss. People could not tell what had happened because the glory had increased. A friend loves at all times (see Prov. 17:17). The love of a friend covers a multitude of faults as the Bible says (see Prov. 10:12). He was being a real friend to me by covering my faults. Beloved, this is why this relationship with Jesus is so important. It will complete you even when you fall short or lack something. Remember, we are completed in Him!

Chapter 7

Jesus' Greatest Goal and Focus in Life "The Right Hand Seat of Intimacy With the Father"

He Appeared Showing Me His Greatest Focus
in Life: "Intimacy with the Father"

The Greatest Place of Closeness

IN ORDER FOR you to understand the impact of all the face-to-face visitations and appearances that are spoken about in this book I must back up. Without telling you in the chronological sequence of how all these things happened I must, from a mature, overall view of understanding, explain the process that the Lord was taking me through. About eight years after my conversion, Jesus appeared to me again, and I had another visitation from God that I didn't understand completely until a few years later as I matured more fully. I really feel the Holy Spirit leading me to share this encounter with you so that you will receive the full impact of the teachings in this book. Our relationship steadily grew deeper as the Lord kept training me, and He began to reveal where this was all leading to.

As I've said before, I didn't understand what He was doing. The Lord started focusing my attention on this passage in Philippians:

> *But what things were gain to me, those I counted loss for Christ....and I count all things but loss for the excellency of the knowledge of Christ Jesus my Lord...* (Philippians 3:7-8).

Notice Paul didn't say anything about counting all things lost for just the *"knowledge"* of Christ, but he referred to gaining the *"excellency"* of the knowledge of Christ. This refers to the highest knowledge of knowing Jesus through an intimate experience.

I Counted All Things Loss

"Honestly, Nothing Meant More"

For years the Holy Spirit led me to these passages of Scripture, and I was so inspired by them, but I did not realize their depth. The Lord was helping to show me. I began counting all things as loss and valuing this pursuit of knowing Him. I began surrendering everything including close relationships in my family, my career, and I was even willing to sacrifice what I wanted in my own life. At a certain point, I didn't have any more ambitions or aspirations. Honestly, nothing else had any value to it compared to finding Him. Before I knew what was going on, I stumbled into a new place with Him where my only aspiration and ambition was to know Him. Knowing Him should also become your sole ambition and desire. This is the highest goal you can aim for. The greatest fulfillment of life is **to know Him!**

The Right Hand Position Seat And Rank

The closest relationship I had ever experienced with the Lord continued to grow for 7 to 8 years when He revealed another aspect of intimacy to me. You see, you do not stay in the same place spiritually year after year. You are either progressing in your relationship with Him, or you are regressing every year. There is no standing still in your relationship with the Lord. The moment you become complacent and neutral (lukewarm; leaving your first love; see Rev. 3:15-16) you lose ground with Him. It is not stressful to be yoked with the Lord in fellowship. I'm not saying that this relationship requires unreasonable stress and a harsh pursuit. It's actually the opposite. Day after day should become more enjoyable, more delightful, and sweeter.

In 1997 I had a visitation from the Lord in which he told me where our relationship had come to. I had asked the Lord to come inspect me, and I was very encouraged by Him concerning the areas of my life and walk that were growing. In spite of all the things that I was falling short in, He revealed to me that I had been promoted to a place with Him in the spirit that I had never heard of nor understood. God has always worked with me in seven-year cycles. If you look over your relationship with God, you may see a similar pattern. I believe that the Lord deals with many of us in seven-year cycles, which means that every seventh year, He completes a chapter or a season in our life and promotes us to the next one. It has been my experience that at the end of a seven-year period, the Lord will give you an assessment of your successes and failures to show you where you stand with Him, as well as show you what you have gained that you can move forward in. It is basically a time of personal promotion. At the time of this visitation, I had been saved for a little more than seven years and had been ministering and preaching on the streets since early in my walk. This was a special time, but I little knew what had taken place spiritually in my walk with God.

MY TRIP TO HEAVEN

The Most Important Appearance From Jesus

A Great Promotion

The first part of this visitation is recorded in Chapters 3 and 4 where I share that God judged me and told me I had slacked in studying His Word. I had entered into a realm with God that I didn't know about, had never heard of, nor knew I could experience. This visitation occurred while I was sleeping. Jesus came to not only let me know what I did wrong by slacking up in spending time with Him in the morning and studying His word long enough, but He also told me that He was promoting me because of my pursuit of Him. He said, *"David, it is one thing for me to bless you, but it is a greater thing for me to give you My right-hand blessing."* Then He said to me, *"You are now one of My right-hand friends."* Then at the end of this visitation, He said, *"There's something about being in right-hand favor and placement with Me!"* Then I woke up. I did not initially understand what He meant by that, but I started studying about the significance of the Lord's right hand of favor. I also began to realize that I had always stood on Jesus' right side when He appeared to me in all of the other visitations. I was standing on Jesus' right side during a visitation at a waterfall. Even during the first part of this visitation when He corrected me, I was still at His right side. When He appeared to me about America, we stood high up in the air and I was standing at His right hand. I wondered what this could all mean.

Our Highest Calling: The Prize

*Brethren, I count not myself to have apprehended: but this one thing I do, forgetting those things which are behind, and **reaching forth unto those things which are before**, I press toward **the mark for the prize of*** *the high calling of God* in *Christ Jesus* (Philippians 3:13-14).

For years I thought and taught that the prize of the high calling of God in Christ Jesus had to do with ministry. I thought it simply meant that if you occupied the office of both apostle and prophet, the greater anointing on your life indicated the higher call you had. But this is not true. After I experienced trips to Heaven and saw the glories of God there, God revealed to me that it meant more than this. Much more!

He Is the Winning Prize

There is a place that we can arrive at in our walk with God that the Bible calls *The Prize*. The prize that Paul spoke of is Jesus—just Jesus. As you study these Scriptures in Philippians, you will notice that Paul initially talks about counting all things that he had gained as a loss so that he could win Christ. Then he talks about pressing toward the mark for the prize of the high calling of God. Prizes are to be reached for; you press on toward them, and you win them. The prize he spoke of winning in this context was Jesus.

He Is the Reward

Winning An Intimacy With Jesus On The Highest Level Possible For All Eternity

That I may win Christ (Philippians 3:8).

He is our reward and prize that we win after all life's accomplishments are over. He's the Reward. This is the same thing the Lord told Abraham, *"I am thy shield, and thy exceeding great reward"* (Gen. 15:1). This refers to winning the Lord in a special, personal relationship. These passages refer to knowing Him on the highest level of closeness. When you have reached this level with God, He will say to you "You have not just sought me and found me, but you have pursued me and given everything up that is valuable and dear to you so that you can have me. And because of this sacrifice, you have won this personal level of intimacy with me." This means that you have been found worthy to know Him intimately.

Winning Jesus

The Holy Spirit (through Paul) said that in order to attain this level of relationship with Him, we must not be distracted by our past, but should reach toward the things in our future. The highest calling we have is to press toward knowing Him. He said that the mark before us that we press toward and look forward to is the highest calling in life and is expressed in His words, *"The high calling of God."* We can know Jesus on this excellent and highest level by giving up everything that means something to us so that we gain Him. Paul said that he did this in order "to know Him" (see Phil 3:10). *"To know Him"* implies being close to Him, and not just knowing Him on any level but also being the closest you can to Him through gaining the excellency of the knowledge about Him!

The Greatest Focus of Jesus' Life

…who for the joy set before Him (Hebrews 12:2).

Jesus' focus was the same. He forgot the things that were behind Him, and reached for the things He saw coming in the future.

> *Looking unto Jesus the author and finisher of our faith;*
> ***who for the joy that was set before him*** *endured the*

*cross, despising the shame, **and is set down at the right*
*hand of the throne God*** (Hebrews 12:2).

Wow! Jesus looked forward to the reward and joy set before
Him. What was this joy He looked forward to in the future? As
you read Scripture, Jesus stated what He looked forward to with
joy especially when being challenged by the religious crowd of His
day saying:

Hereafter shall the Son of man sit on the right hand of the
power of God (Luke 22:69).

He referred several times to looking forward to His future
prize and reward for His service and sacrifice. This was His vision
and focus. Jesus didn't just want to sit in a position of authority
enthroned next to God the Father, but He wanted to sit close to the
father in the right-hand chair. Jesus' greatest goal and focus in life
wasn't to sit next to God for the motive of position and power in
His Kingdom, but to have intimacy with the Father. The right-hand
position is the most close and intimate place that you can have with
the King in His sovereign realm. Jesus' pursuit in life was intimacy
with God. The winning prize and reward in Jesus' Life was to know
His Father in the most intimate way and He attained this when He
sat down at His Father's right hand. Now the Father tells us that
our pursuit in life should be intimacy with His Son. The Bible tells
us that when we focus on winning Jesus, the Father will notice our
love.

Jesus Admonishes Us to Have His Joy

The Bible says that Jesus' joy was pursuing intimacy with the
Father, and He encouraged us to have His joy. In different places
in Scripture, Jesus mentions that His joy will make our joy full and

complete (see John 16:22). There's a difference in His joy and our joy.

> These things have I spoken unto you, that **my joy** might remain in you, and that **your joy** might be full (John 15:11).

Many Christians (and sinners) do not experience complete joy because they don't know the Lord's personal joy, nor does it remain in them. Jesus prayed to the Father that His personal joy would fulfill us!

> ...that they might have My joy fulfilled in themselves (John 17:13).

Hebrews tells us that there was a joy that Jesus had set before Himself, which must refer to being seated at the right hand of God. The Scripture also declares:

> In His presence is fulness of joy and at His right hand pleasures forevermore (Psalm 16:11).

This Scripture mentions joy, and in the same breath mentions the Lord's right hand. This should also be our joy, and the Lord wants us to enter into His joy (see Matt. 25:21).

Desiring to Sit at the Right Hand

"The Eternal Position for All Time"

Sitting at the right hand of God is a position of power, but it is obtained through pure motives of the heart in wanting to be close to God. It is not obtained because of prideful desires for a position of power. One must be motivated by the place that the seat is in and not so much the position and power that the seat gives. Jesus was motivated by where the seat was at (near the Father) and not by His desire for power. This word *"right hand"* comes from the Greek word *"dexios"* which means, *"A place of honor, favor, and thus being a position of power and authority."*[1] To sit at someone's right hand is a position of honor and closeness, and it is the highest position of intimacy that a person can gain in the Father's Kingdom.

The greatest honor that Jesus could receive in Heaven was to sit at the right hand of the father and be ever close at His side. This was Christ's focus and goal while He lived on Earth. He wanted to be close to the Father, and not just earn a position of authority with Him. This is the difference between satan and Jesus. Lucifer wanted a higher position of authority, and he thought it robbery to be equal with God, so he strived to overthrow God to get it. Lucifer didn't just want the right-hand seat next to God, which resulted in being close to Him, but instead he wanted God's throne and position of authority itself. You need to understand that satan knew about this right-hand seat, and he bypassed it because He wanted God's throne and place (see Isa. 14:13-14). Jesus was in the beginning with God, and He saw lucifer fall from Heaven like lightning. This also had to mean that lucifer saw Him and the glory that Jesus Himself spoke of having with the Father in the beginning (see John 17:5; 23-24).

His Greatest Goal: The Right-Hand Seat of Intimacy and Power

Jesus also had this right-hand position of glory in the beginning when He was with God. Jesus did not focus on His exaltation, power, authority, or the Kingdom that was given to Him more than He focused on the intimacy He had with God. All those things were secondary to Him compared to His close and intimate seat next to God. Even though Jesus gained a new Kingdom and received glory,

He never speaks about these things being His focus. His focus was to be near God

The Seat Versus the Throne

What made Jesus great in God's eyes is that He was humble enough to choose the seat versus the throne, and because of this God exalted Jesus to sit with Him on His Throne. Jesus didn't teach us what He did not first live Himself. He told us in parabolic form to always choose the low seat when we are invited to sit among many seats.

> *When thou art bidden of any man to a wedding, **sit not down in the highest room**; lest a more honourable man than thou be bidden of him....But when thou art bidden, **go and sit down in the lowest room**; that when he that bade thee cometh, he may say unto thee, Friend, go up higher: **then shalt thou have worship in the presence of them that sit at meat with thee.** For whosoever exalteth himself shall be abased; and **he that humbleth himself shall be exalted** (Luke 14:8,10-11).*

When I first got saved I thought that Jesus was just teaching us how we are to live. I never thought about how this might apply to His own life. But no, it was more than this! He was teaching us how He lived and wanted us to follow His example. He made the seat His focus and not God's throne. This right-hand seat is the lowest seat, but it is also the highest seat. God the Father allowed Jesus to sit with Him in His throne.

> *To him that overcometh will I grant to sit with me in my throne, **even as I also overcame, and am set down with my Father in his throne** (Revelation 3:21).*

Because humanity has a hard time understanding the greatness of God's kingdom, we don't understand the great honor Jesus meant by this. To sit with a king in his throne is a great honor and was something that lucifer tried to rob for. Heaven sees this right-hand position of closeness as greater than if we were to attain our own personal throne. This is what Jesus meant by the reward. He promised that He would allow those who overcome to sit with Him in His throne like He sat with His Father in His Father's throne. This is one of the greatest honors one can ever have in all of Heaven. Satan killed and pridefully destroyed to take this place, but Jesus humbly submitted to the Father's will.

Seated in Heavenly Places: Ambition or Intimacy?

Rick Joyner shares a trip he took to Heaven in his book, *The Final Quest.*[2] In this book Rick shares that he saw some of the greatest preachers and servants of God in Heaven who had received honor from men while they lived on earth. When some of these preachers reached eternity, they occupied some of the lowest places in Heaven and did not sit at the right hand of God and make it to the highest calling of God in Christ. As I read his book, I was shocked to hear Rick share that he had seen some of the greatest people and ministries denied a position next to Jesus for all eternity. Some of these ministries and people had impacted the world and had won many souls to the Lord but were denied the seat next to Jesus for all eternity. As Rick spoke to some of them, they shared their many failings with him. Some confessed that they had not allowed the Lord to judge their character while they lived on the earth. You must repent before you die! Change cannot be made after you exit the earth or this life.

Some didn't win Christ on this level because they failed to walk in love with their fellow ministers or brothers and sisters. Instead they became jealous and threatened by the accomplishments of others. Some operated in insecurity, which caused them to compete with others in ministry. And others failed because of lust, perversion, and, most of all, because of pride. Pride, high-mindedness, and arrogance were some of the main reasons many didn't make it. I didn't know that so many of the great people who reformed the church and changed world history failed because they didn't allow their own soul to be reformed. I didn't know that you could reform the world without reforming you own soul. This can result in all your accomplishments being vain before God!

Wouldn't You Rather Know Now Than Later?

You see, God's judgments are different from ours. He doesn't judge what way we do as much as He judges our heart, motives, and character! I began to realize that many who missed the great opportunity to sit next to Jesus for all eternity did so because they didn't walk in love or remain devoted to Jesus alone. Reading this book changed my life and served to confirm that the appearance I had concerning the right-hand position was true. Those who had overcome and remained faithful to God, however, were able to enjoy this honor in Heaven.

They worshiped the Lord and followed Him wherever He went and did not deviate from this lifestyle! I realized that at times I had been distracted from this path of devotion. God used Rick's book to encourage me to stay on this journey of love toward the Lord. The blessings and judgments of the Lord are what keep us on the path to life. Many who erred in Heaven from this great place erred because they never asked the Lord to judge them before they died. You see, you can ask the Lord to judge your life in the here and now, and He will. This is also scriptural. You can stand before the judgment seat of Christ now, while you are alive, or later at the end of your life when you die. It's better to be judged now than later as judgment prepares you to be eligible for Heaven. The results of this are a beautiful thing, although it may sound scary! I've experienced it in Heaven before Jesus' seat and you can have this too. This in turn will prepare you for the awesome glories of Heaven for all eternity!

The High Calling of God Is Attained in This World but Gained in Eternity

In his trip to Heaven, Rick Joyner passed by many great men who started major movements and denominations in the Lord's name. Because they didn't deal with pride before the end of their life, these saints disqualified themselves from sitting at God's right hand and fulfilling the high calling of God. He also saw great writers and prominent people of history who were disqualified from sitting in this place of closeness and power next to Jesus because of their attitudes, character, and lack of love toward others. As Jesus walked Rick by His throne, Rick noticed that the majority of those who sat at His right hand and had been found faithful were housewives. They sat in the most prestigious place in Heaven.

I was shocked as I read that God told Rick that all our accomplishments would be in vain if they aren't done for the sake of loving Him and His cross. The most unlikely people here on earth, who are despised and overlooked, are honored and glorious in Heaven because of their humility and love. Rick observed that there were still many vacant seats next to Jesus that could have been filled in any generation, but they remained empty. I ask you now, beloved reader, will you be one of them? You can be! Rick noticed a special man who had been arrayed in glory and was sitting in one of these special right-hand seats.

This was the greatest story of this book! Rick asked what this man had done to earn such an honor. This man had been a homeless Christian, what people in this world would call a bum, who had lived on the streets. Jesus shared with Rick that mainstream churches had rejected this man because he was dressed poorly. He used all the love that he had developed toward the Lord, which was small in comparison to some of us in the church who have developed more through the knowledge of God's word. He also became a minister of the gospel on the streets among the homeless people. Jesus explained to Rick how the mainstream Church of today rejected this man because he wasn't dressed properly or polished in ministry like the great ministers in the cathedrals of our time. He was one who had won this place next to the Lord. He had only gotten one person saved. Rick initially thought that this man had won many souls to the Lord to earn this place of honor, but it turned out that he had not done any great ministry or won thousands to the Lord like some of the prominent ministers Rick had already seen. This man had only won one person to the Lord. Jesus shared that this man had seen another man freezing to death on the street. It was a very cold winter night, and he knew this man would die if he didn't keep warm, so he wrapped his body around this man all night to keep him warm. The man he kept warm survived, but he died. This homeless man displayed such compassion and, out of love, he gave up his life for another. Many of those who sit at God's right hand are there because of their acts of love.

The main reason that the people made it to the right hand of the Father was because they walked in love toward the Lord and other people.

Jesus did the same for us—He died just so we could live and be seated where He is seated, at the right hand of the Father. Love is the key! A love that is stronger than death or the fear of dying! How amazing! Anyone reading this book can sit in this place of honor, but you must pursue Him—not fame, a huge ministry, or success! Just Him! He alone must be your focus! Never deviating from loving Jesus with all your heart, body, mind, and soul is the key!

"You Too Can Have the Place of Closeness Seated Next to Jesus at God's Right Hand"

Paul encourages us in Colossians to look forward to and seek after Heavenly things instead of setting our affections and aspirations on earthly, material things.

> *If ye then be risen with Christ, seek those things which are above, where Christ sitteth on the right hand of God. Set your affection on things above, not on things on the earth* (Colossians 3:1-2).

Here God gives us the invitation and admonishment to seek and look for those things which are above. Where do we look to? To the right hand where Christ sits, which is a place of friendship, closeness, and the highest level of intimacy we can have with the Lord Jesus and His Father. Do you see this? The Bible didn't say it was wrong or ambitious to seek, press, and strive for those things that are at the right hand of God. Some of us have had the mindset that to seek to sit at the Lord's right hand is a prideful and ambitious thing because of what the mother of James and John ambitiously desired of Jesus (see Matt. 4:21).

> *Then came to Him the mother of Zebedees children with her sons, worshipping Him, and desiring a thing of Him. And he said unto her, What wilt thou? She said unto him, Grant that these my two sons may sit, the one on thy right hand, and the other on the left, in thy kingdom* (Matthew 20:20-21).

She asked that her sons, James and John, sit at His right and left hand. She didn't truly understand what she was asking:

> *...Ye know not what ye ask* (Matthew 20:22).

This request was also born out of a mother's ambition to see her sons gain authority in Jesus' kingdom and not out of relationship. But you also need to understand that this request wouldn't have been possible had Jesus not already given some teaching about His kingdom and introduced that you could sit at the right hand of the Father. We see that Jesus did teach on this later in Luke 22:29-30. Jesus encouraged this by being the primary example Himself and stating that His aspiration was to sit at the hand of God and power.

We are commanded and admonished to seek those things that are in Heaven, where Christ sits at the right hand of God. When many people think of Heaven above, they only want to see the mansion that the Lord is building for them. Others may think about walking on the streets of gold or about their different rewards for serving in this life. The priority of some is to be reunited with loved ones, while others consider the eternal bliss of immortality. All these things are wonderful, but they are not Him nor do they promote intimacy with the Lord. This is why the Bible admonishes us that we are to seek "those things" at the right hand of God where Christ sits. At His right hand, there is a place of intimacy, and above all there are pleasures there with Him forevermore!

> ...*at thy right hand there are pleasures for evermore*
> (Psalm 16:11).

The Bible also speaks that there are *"things"* at this right hand place where Christ sits. You must find out what these *things* are! In this friendship and place of intimacy and power with God come many things. Even though this place is a position of power, this wasn't Jesus' ambition in looking forward to the seat next to God. Jesus was motivated by love in seeking to sit closest to His Father. We are also invited by Jesus to make this our life's aim and goal!

The Father Makes This Call

But the striking thing is that Jesus said that He does not decide who can sit at his right or left side:

> *But to sit on my right hand, and on my left, is not mine to give, but it shall be given to them for whom it is prepared of my Father* (Matthew 20:23).

This Place Is Prepared for Us by the Father

Jesus answers the woman who asked that Jesus promote her sons to his right and left side. He lets her know that it isn't His call to make and that He does not have the authority to make this decision—only the Father decides who sits at the right and left hand of Jesus. It was the Father's decision to give this place to man just as He decided to put Jesus at His own right hand (see Eph. 1:20). Jesus' rank and authority is not the same as the Father's:

> *...for my Father is greater than I* (John 14:28).

Jesus tells us that there are some things that the Father alone holds in His hands.

> *It is not for you to know the times or the seasons, which the Father hath put in his own power* (Acts 1:7).

> *But of that day in that hour knoweth no man, no, not the angels, which are in Heaven, neither the Son, but the Father* (Mark 13:32).

Then I remembered Philippians 3:14:

> *I press toward the mark for the prize of the high calling of God in Christ Jesus.*

The calling and invitation to sit at His right hand was not from Jesus, but from God the Father! The Father has prepared this place for us. Just as He prepared this place for His Son, He's also prepared this place for us to sit at!

Will You Be One of Them?

It's Prepared for You: "Will You Win Him?"

But to sit on my right hand, and on my left, is not mine to give, but it shall be given to them for whom it is prepared of my Father (Matthew 20:23).

Notice that Jesus said the Father will prepare this place for **them!"** Many will answer this high call from God. What is that call? God's call in this life is for us to strive to gain the excellency of the knowledge of His Son Jesus. He's looking to see if we will be found worthy to win Jesus in the most intimate relationship we can have. This is a call from God to love His Son, hear His Son, and pursue relationship with His Son.

He that hath my commandments, and keepeth them, he it is that loveth me: and he that loveth me shall be loved of my Fathe…Jesus answered and said unto him, If a man love me, he will keep my words: and my Father will love him… (John 14:21-23).

*And there came a voice out of the cloud, saying, **This is my beloved Son: hear him*** (Luke 9:35).

We love the Son before we love the Father and when we love Jesus, the Father is pleased. This intimacy experience with Jesus is beyond ecstasy and the knowledge of all other things. The Father's heart is for us to first know His Son.

> *Then said they unto him, Where is thy Father? Jesus answered, Ye neither know me, nor my Father:* ***if ye had known me, ye should have known my Father also*** *(John 8:19).*

> *That all men should honour the Son, even as they honour the Father.* ***He that honoureth not the Son honoureth not the Father which hath sent him*** *(John 5:23).*

He puts His Son first; then in turn, Jesus responds with love by putting Him first and telling us about the Father and revealing Him.

> *...neither knoweth any man the Father, save the Son, and He to whomsoever the Son will reveal him* (Matthew 11:27).

The Highest Call in Life Is Loving Jesus

The whole purpose in writing this book is to show you what the Lord has for us. The whole purpose of life is to have this type of relationship with Jesus. This is an intimacy beyond the ecstasy of this world. I've experienced it, and now I want you to have the same. You can have this relationship with Him too! When Jesus walked me around Heaven and showed me all these right-hand seats next to Him and the Father, I saw how majorly the Church missed the focus and point of the Lord's heart.

It is important for you to realize that this type of intimacy is waiting for you on the other side of this life. You must establish it here in this lifetime by sacrificing everything that stands in the way of your intimacy with the Lord. You must be willing to give up all valuable things so that they do not hinder you from obtaining this intimate place next to Him. It's not about the sacrifice. Don't focus on what you have to give up. It is about loving Him, and if you love Him, the sacrifice will feel like a small thing you can do. Love is stronger than death and stronger than sacrifice (see Song of Sol. 8:6). Our highest calling in life is to love Jesus.

Once Gained, Intimacy Shall Never Be Taken Away

> But one thing is needful: and Mary hath chosen that good part, **which shall not be taken away from her** (Luke 10:42).

Mary had an intimate relationship with God and she spent time at His feet. He promises her and us that this type of intimacy will never be taken away! Listen to what Jesus said to Rick Joyner when he was taken to Heaven:

> You are an earthen vessel, and that is all that you will be while you walk the earth. However, you can see Me just as clearly there (earth) as you do here, if you will look with the eyes of your heart. You can be just as close to Me there as anyone has ever been to Me, and even more so. I have made the way for everyone to be as close to Me as they truly desire to be. If you really desire to be even closer to Me than Paul was, you can. Some will want this, and they will want it badly enough to lay aside anything that hinders their intimacy with Me to give themselves fully to it and they will have what they seek.

If it is your quest to walk there just as you can walk with Me here, I will be just as close to you there as I am now. If you seek Me, you will find Me. If you draw near to Me, I will draw near to you. It is My desire to set a table for you right in the midst of your enemies. This is not just My desire for My leaders, but for all who call upon My name. I want to be much closer to you, and to everyone who calls upon Me, than I have yet been able to be with anyone who has lived. You determine how close we will be, not I. I will be found by those who seek Me.[3]

That I May Know Him

What Our Real Boast Should Be About Concerning the Lord

That I may know Him (Philippians 3:10).

To Know Him

We shouldn't boast about our spiritual gifts, our spiritual wealth, the anointing, material things we have, or any of these fleeting things. He is eternal and will last forever! We should boast in knowing Jesus as a close and personal friend. We shouldn't be prideful about the areas we are mighty or possess strength in.

> *But he that truly boast or rejoice let him rejoice in the fact that God says, He knoweth me. Thus saith the Lord, **Let not the wise man glory in his wisdom, neither let the mighty man glory in his might, let not the rich man glory in his riches: But let him that glorieth glory in this, that he understandeth and knoweth***

me, that I am the Lord which exercise lovingkindness, judgment, and righteousness, in the earth: for in these things I delight, saith the Lord (Jeremiah 9:23-24).

This has been God's cry throughout history and to Israel down through the years: *"I desired...the knowledge of God more than burnt offerings"* (Hos. 6:6). The Lord was upset with Israel because there was no knowledge of Him in the land (see Hos. 4:1). He wants us to know Him. This was Paul's greatest cry and the Lord wants this to be our greatest cry. Oh, *"that I may know Him!"* (see Phil. 3:10). To know Him should be our greatest boast, glory, and praise!

"After All This...There's Still More!"

God the Father will not permit us to pursue intimacy with Him before we gain intimacy with Jesus. Jesus Himself has won this place of intimacy with God the Father, and the Father commands us to believe, receive, and love His Son before coming to Him. The Father was so pleased that Jesus pursued intimacy with the Father and obeyed His will through suffering for all humankind. As a result, the Lord promoted Jesus to the highest place of intimacy in His kingdom. Our job is to pursue this intimacy with Jesus. As we gain this place of intimacy with Jesus, we automatically win what He has already won, including intimacy with His Father.

Now the Lord was introducing me to the intimacy with the Father before I realized it. I had fallen so deeply in love with Jesus that I didn't know that there was another level of intimacy with the Godhead. The Lord told me that I had come to a place where I had loved Him at such a great level that it had touched His heart in a special way. He then said, *"Now, I will reveal My Father to you. David, He is My greatest pursuit in life even now. This is My greatest prize and reward."* Then He said, with such loving tenderness in His voice, *"Just Him."* I knew He was talking about the Father and winning an intimate relationship with Him in Person. He then continued, *"I still pursue, follow, and obey My Father's commands and desires today."* As Jesus stood in front of me I saw such regal, reverential honor and love for His Father. I also knew that the Father loved Him deeply, and I was about to see it firsthand.

Chapter 8

JESUS INTRODUCES ME TO THE FATHER IN PERSON

"Jesus Shows Me His Life's Greatest Desire"

Jesus Reveals Who His Father Was to Me

ONE NIGHT, DURING a seven-day, shut-in fast inside the church, I had one of the most thrilling experiences I've ever had with the Lord. It was late, and I was up reading and studying the Lord's word when Jesus suddenly appeared in front of me. The door was shut, and I didn't see Him walk through the door as I had seen him do at other times. He just appeared in front of me as I sat after a time during my worship adoration and study with Him. Jesus looked very glorious as He normally did when I saw Him. He then said to me, *"David, the covenant I made with you years ago in Heaven—that both My Father and I will now come down to Earth to work with you personally like we did with Moses—is about to take place on Earth. I will now reveal who My Father is to you, and now He Himself will also work with you!"*

I had always wondered about Jesus' promise:

> *He that hath my commandments, and keepeth them, he it*
> *is that loveth me: and* **he that loveth me shall be loved**
> **of my Father, and I will love him, and will manifest**
> **myself to him**....*Jesus answered and said unto him, If*
> *a man love me, he will keep my words:* **and my Father**
> **will love him, and we will come unto him,** *and make*
> *our abode with him* (John 14:21,23).

Jesus mentions a few verses later that, if we keep loving Him, both He and His Father will come and make their habitation and living quarters in our lives.

I knew this was the next level that Jesus was taking me to as I had read that *"No man cometh unto the Father, but by me"* (John 14:6). The words, *"But by Me"* implies an exception, and Jesus is the exception. The Bible also says that Jesus is the only one who has the power to show the Father to us.

> *That thou keep this commandment without spot, unrebuk-*
> *able, until the appearing of our Lord Jesus Christ: Which*
> *in his times he shall shew, who is the blessed and only*
> *Potentate, the King of kings, and Lord of lords; Who only*
> *hath immortality, dwelling in the light which no man can*
> *approach unto; whom no man hath seen, nor can see: to*
> *whom be honor and power everlasting. Amen* (1 Timothy
> 6:14-16).

I was enjoying the awesome face-to-face relationship I had with Jesus, so this came as a surprise! I didn't really know that there was something or someone greater to meet beyond Jesus—the Father. Jesus said, *"Let me introduce you to My Father."* In this statement, Jesus wanted to introduce me to the Father, and I saw how the God-head lives their Word: *"Let another man praise thee, and not thine own mouth; a stranger, and not thine own lips"* (Prov. 27:2). Each person in the trinity does not talk about themselves, but rather speaks of the others instead.

We can see this in the Bible when the Holy Spirit doesn't speak about Himself, but always gives reference to Jesus and glorifies Him. Jesus never talks about Himself but gives witness to the Father or the Holy Spirit. Then, in turn, the Father makes reference to His Son and His Holy Spirit. It is awesome! With this, Jesus took me on a journey to meet His Father in Heaven. *"You must know and understand the one you are working with,"* said Jesus. I had walked with Jesus for 16 solid years at this point, and had experienced face-to-face appearances from Jesus that led to intimate fellowship. And now He was introducing me to His Father. To My Father! To my God! With this, we ascended to His throne. I say ascended because God's throne sits in an elevated place and everything leads up to it. We passed by the four beautiful beasts with four faces, and they were powerful in appearance. They were crying in reverence about how Holy the Father is.

He Was Glorious and Enthroned in Majesty Above

We passed the sea of glass that is present before the Great Throne of God. It was pure as crystal. It was as pure as a translucent diamond. God the Father has this awesome beautiful sea that His throne overlooks, and it is so gorgeous. It is like looking out a window from the second floor of your home and seeing a beautiful pond in your backyard, except that the sea of glass is a billion times more beautiful! In my first book, *Face-to-Face Appearances From Jesus,* I share about a trip I took to see waterfalls in Jesus' backyard. After I saw the glass sea, I began to understand why. The Father loves to be around water just like Jesus does. We bypassed the seats that the twenty-four elders sat on. These elders have gold crowns on their heads. There was electricity, lightning, thunder, and voices coming out of His throne that were so powerful! The sound of all this energy and power coming from His throne created an atmosphere of reverence and the fear of God. It was like the noise of a billion locomotive freight trains combined with the deep roar of a trillion tornadoes with lightning and crackling. It sounded like popping thunder during an electrical storm. It was so beautifully terrifying. It was an awesome sight! This explained what I had always wondered about in Scripture:

> *And out of the throne proceeded lightnings and thunderings and voices...* (Revelation 4:5).

> *...the Lord will come down in the sight of all the people upon mount Sinai* (Exodus 19:11).

> *And it came to pass on the third day in the morning, that there were thunders and lightnings, and a thick cloud upon the mount, and the voice of the trumpet exceeding loud; so that all the people that was in the camp trembled* (Exodus 19:16).

> *And all the people saw the thunderings, and the lightnings, and the noise of the trumpet, and the mountain smoking: and when the people saw it, they removed, and stood afar off* (Exodus 20:18).

I had read that even in Moses time, thunder and lightning accompanied the Father's presence when He came down in the sight of all the people. If you study biblical history, you will find that when the Father manifested Himself, electricity, lightning, thunder, earthquakes, precious stones, voices, brilliant light, and fire were always the trademarks of the Father's presence and glory. The Father is so beautiful and now I was getting a chance to look upon Him more plainly. I saw the Father on the throne with a wedding band on His finger while I was prostrate before Him. In this visitation, the light coming from the Father was so brilliant coming from the Father, that I could only see His hands, legs, and feet while I lay facedown on the beautiful marble floor surrounding His throne.

Jesus Reveals the Father's Glory to Me

"The More Excellent Glory"

For he received from God the Father honour and glory, **when there came such a voice to him from the excellent glory...** (2 Peter 1:17).

His body looked like a billion brilliant diamonds and precious stones coordinating together in a lovely way as they seemed to be implanted into His very being. As I looked closely, His body was changing colors because the reflections of light were changing within the stones. He was brilliantly gorgeous! Now I know what Ezekiel and the apostle John meant when they described the Father:

And above the firmament that was over their heads was the likeness of a throne, as the appearance of a sapphire stone: and upon the likeness of the throne was the likeness as the appearance of a man above upon it (Ezekiel 1:26).

And immediately I was in the spirit: and, behold, a throne was set in heaven, and one sat on the throne. **And he that sat was to look upon like a jasper and a sardine stone:** *and there was a rainbow round about the throne, in sight like unto an emerald* (Revelation 4:2-3).

Moses also spoke of precious stones:

And they saw the God of Israel: and there was under his feet as it were a paved work of a sapphire

stone, and as it were the body of heaven in his clearness (Exodus 24:10).

These stones and diamonds that reflected and radiated so much light were brilliant and blinding so that I could not move any closer to the Father without Jesus strengthening me and carrying me the rest of the way toward Him. Now I know what that Scripture means when it says that, *"No man cometh to the Father, but by me"* (John 14:6). The other interesting thing that I hadn't noticed before is that the Father's throne is moveable and transportable. The throne He sits on is a moveable throne like an ancient throne that is carried by four men.

His throne had wheels on it, and the four beasts were the ones who carried Him on this beautiful, white throne. This throne was beautiful! I found out later that the Scriptures record this to be true.

> **...the Ancient of days did sit**, *whose garment was white as snow, and the hair of his head like the pure wool: his throne was like the fiery flame,* **and his wheels as burning fire** (Daniel 7:9).

> **And when the living creatures went, the wheels went by them**: *and when the living creatures were lift up from the earth, the wheels were lifted up. Whithersoever the spirit was to go, they went, thither was their spirit to go; and the wheels were lifted up over against them:* **for the spirit of the living creature was in the wheels** (Ezekiel 1:19-20).

I was basking in the glory of God, but there was a deep sense of reverence all around me and in me for who I was seeing and what I was seeing. He was fiery in appearance—a beautiful fire with the same form and likeness of a man inside it. Now I understood when the Lord said in the Bible, *"Let Us make man in our image and after Our likeness"* (Gen. 1:26). We are made in the image and the likeness of God!

He's a Spirit Man of Fire

The only way I can describe this fire is to say that it is sort of like the brilliance of the sun, but it is a trillion times brighter! Our human bodies could not take such light and glory. The only way I could was because the Lord had taken my spirit out of my body into Heaven to see this. Fire leaped off the Father in gushes like fire leaps off the sun and into space for miles. This is what Israel saw when the Father descended upon Mt. Sinai with fire. The Father is a Man of Fire. He has the appearance of blazing fire in the form of a man, but a very real Person is behind all of this brilliant burning. He's not just any fire, but a consuming fire that leaps onto everything around Him. Anything He touches is fully enveloped in fire and combusts. He consumes everything that is in His path. This is why the Lord warned Israel to avoid coming too close to the mountain when He came down upon it. The Father explained to Moses that He would break forth on the people and consume them when they gazed in amazement and came too close and broke the boundaries the Father had set. He didn't want the Israelites to cross boundaries and come too close. Have you ever noticed that people stand far away when a building is burning with blazing fire? The Bible also records this to be true:

> *And I saw as the color of amber, as the appearance of fire round about within it,* ***from the appearance of his loins even upward, and from the appearance of his loins even downward, I saw as it were the appearance of fire****, and it had brightness round about* (Ezekiel 1:27).

*And mount Sinai was altogether on a smoke, **because the Lord descended upon it in fire**: and the smoke thereof ascended as the smoke of a furnace, and the whole mount quaked greatly* (Exodus 19:18).

For our God is a consuming fire (Hebrews 12:29).

*And let the priests also, which come near to the Lord, sanctify themselves, **lest the Lord break forth upon them*** (Exodus 19:22).

I also felt a powerful, magnetic pull in the atmosphere around us.

His Powerful, Magnetic Attraction

I then began to understand Scriptures that refer to the Father's character: *"No man can come to me, except the Father...draw him"* (John 6:44). The Father has a magnetic drawing and pull in His presence and Person. This is also the same drawing power that Jesus mentions (see John 12:32). The Father was magnetic and mesmerizing! I then began to understand the science of the gravitational pull of the sun that keeps all the planets in orbit and in a delicate balance. Our Father is powerful and He is so big! He was gigantic in this visitation! The Father was big and He was complete fire and light, but His presence was full of love! He was astonishing! He was breathtaking! He was awesome! Then Jesus said to me, *"This is My Father. He won't hurt you; He loves you. Fear not!"* Jesus knew I was feeling great reverence and godly fear. I was so afraid, but in a pure way, as Jesus brought me before Him. Now I understand why Peter, James, and John were afraid when the Father came down on the mount of transfiguration (see Luke 9:34).

The Father is *awesome*, and He carries an atmosphere of reverence wherever He resides. I was awestricken! I could sense that there was mercy around Jesus that would cover mistakes and errors. Now that Jesus was introducing me to His Father, I felt the weight of His glory and character in a different way than I had experienced before. It dawned on me why Jesus said, *"My Father... is greater than all..."* (John 10:29). I saw His glory. It was the more excellent glory that Peter talked about when he saw the Father's glory on the mount of transfiguration with Jesus (see 2 Pet. 1:17-18). The Father has a more excellent glory that surpasses even Jesus' glory and the glory of the Holy Spirit! That is why the Scripture says that it is more excellent. If the Father's glory and majesty wasn't more excellent then the Bible wouldn't say that it was. The Father was remarkable and majestic when I saw Him. Since this first time I met the Father, I have seen Him many times and He is always sitting on a royal throne. You are mistaken if you think that there is no rank within the Godhead!

Jehovah God was in front of me, but I couldn't see His face. He allowed me to draw close to Him as much as I could, but the power, light, and glory from His presence were too overwhelming so that I was only able to come to His feet. Jesus was standing next to me, and He helped me to endure the glory coming from His Father.

The Father Loves Worship

When I got as close as I could to the Father, I saw that He loves and longs to be worshipped and adored in a certain way. As I observed Him and His character, I realized that He wanted more than just praise. He longed to be reverenced, adored, worshipped, and honored. It was beyond praise! He desired true worship manifested in spirit and in truth. I saw worship going on around His throne from the four beasts, the twenty-four elders, and the hosts of Heaven. He desired worship with reverence. There were clouds and smoke around Him. Lightning and thunder poured forth out of His throne as the worship ascended unto Him which came from the hosts of Heaven.

Approaching the Almighty God: Jehovah

No man cometh unto the Father, but by Me (John 14:6).

Jesus Brings Me to the Father

Friends, I first passed by the light that is more brilliant than a billion suns that surrounds Him. I moved past the fog of His glory, past the clouds, mist, and the blazing, consuming fire that was leaping off of Him. I continued on beyond the lightning and crackling thunder that proceeded out of His throne and seemed to surround Him. I walked by the four beautiful beasts that were crying noisily, "Holy, Holy, Holy is the Lord God Almighty who was, who is, and who is to come!" These angels had beautiful wings and their collective voices sounded like the voice of the Almighty and resembled the sound of many waters, oceans, and seas. I moved past the beautiful crystal-glass sea that extends before His throne. I passed through all of the glory that was surrounding Him and by the twenty-four elders that worship before His throne, until I saw Him. After I passed through all of this, I saw Him as a person.

Being Introduced to the Father

Jesus' eyes were flames of fire. He took me through all of these external components of the Father, inside and beyond, to show me Him. We passed all this and when the Father let me inside, there He was. I stood there with just Jesus and the Father. The Father was love, and He was a friend. The Father took me past all of these wonderful outward manifestations of His presence and allowed me to see His personality. He is a Person. Then the voice of the Almighty started speaking saying,

> *I've brought you past all these aspects concerning Me that some never get past their whole life while on earth to see- ing or understanding Me as a Person or Friend. I, your Father, also desire David, to be man's friend. I am your Friend. You have touched the heart of Me by wanting to be close to Me like you have. You have pursued me and my ultimate friendship, and now you have found Me and won me as a friend. I now give you this charge to go and bring more of your brothers and sisters to this place of knowing Me in person as Friend, beyond the exterior and outward Light and manifestation of My glory. This is the greatest honor anyone could have with Me, David, not to know Me just as Father, King, Savior, Emperor, God, or Lord, but as Friend. I now charge you to go and bring forth fruit in this area!*

Suddenly, the Father showed me this beautiful seat that was next to Jesus. The seat was at His right hand and among many oth- ers. It was so beautiful and glorious! Then the voice of the Father spoke and said, *"Because of your love for My Son you have also touched Me and I have prepared this seat of the right-hand next to Him for all eter- nity reserved in Heaven just for you."* I knew that this was the same right-hand seat that was shown to me by Jesus from the visitation that I already described to you previously which took place in 1997. It was now a few years later and the Lord was showing me this right hand seat of intimacy next to Jesus for the second time, but this time by the Father Himself. I was happy to see it again.

After He finished talking, I was carried back through the bril- liant light, glory, fire, electricity, and lightning. We continued back through the thunder, the sounds of voices, cries of beauty, and through the indescribable brilliance that surrounds Him. Then He revealed the Scripture to me that, "He is the only one having immortality dwelling in the light which no man can approach unto." He's not all those things that surround His throne or His body. The Father Himself dwells within the light and no one can approach Him unless Jesus takes them.

Behind the Light of His Immortality and Glory

I could not approach the Father by myself. Jesus had to personally take me behind the veil of these things that surround the Father so that I could see the more intimate side of who He really is in Person. He is love and He is a friend to me. As we walked back to the outer realms of this glory that was emanating from the Father's presence, Jesus began to speak to me, but it was like the Father was speaking prophetically through Him in a first person voice: *"This is what We were to Adam before the fall. Adam experienced Me like this, David. Now you can because of the blood covenant that My Son made through His cross."*

Somehow, even though Jesus was talking, it was like the Father was prophetically speaking through His Voice in first person, as Jesus and I walked back to the outer realms of this glory emanating from the Father's presence. Then this Scripture became even more illuminated when Jesus said that, *"No man can come unto God except by Me"* (see John 14:6). It was Jesus that made it possible for us to have this relationship with the Father. Because of sin, we could no longer experience or enjoy His presence like Adam and Eve did in the Garden. Jesus came to restore our way back into the Almighty's presence.

The Almighty God and Father of our Lord Jesus Christ called me friend and His chosen! You too can have this experience! You can also have this special life that is marked by supernatural encounters and visitations with Jesus and the Father! This dimension is not just a relationship, but it is life! It's the abundant life with God in Person. For years I had loved Jesus intensely. I had endured His chastisement and because of this, I made a decision to not cool off toward Him. The Lord dealt with me as a son. He matured me. I moved into Sonship with Him by going through His judgments. While Jesus was doing this in my life through these appearances, He was preparing me to stand before the Father! The Lord has dealt with me as a son. He has matured me.

Eight Years of Bliss With the Father

So He moved me into the next experience and level of relationship with His Father beyond where I had been with Him as the Son of God. I did not know that it could get any greater, but for the next eight years, I would start to have continual encounters, not only with Jesus face to face but now also with the Father. They had both come to make their abode and living arrangements with me as Jesus had said in the book of John:

> *Jesus answered and said unto him, If a man love me, he will keep my words: and **my Father will love him, and we will come unto him, and make our abode with him*** (John 14:23).

To be continued...

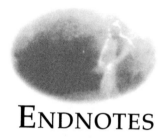

ENDNOTES

Chapter 1

1. Strong's Concordance, "mathetas," #3101, www.eliyah.com/lexicon.html.

2. Strong's Concordance, "austeros," #840, www.eliyah.com/lexicon.html.

3. Strong's Concordance, "agonizomai," #75, www.eliyah.com/lexicon.html.

4. Strong's Concordance, "zeteo," #2212, www.eliyah.com/lexicon.html.

5. Rick Renner, *Sparkling Gems from the Greek* (Dayton, OH: Teach All Nations, Publisher, 2003).

6. Strong's Concordance, "zealous," www.eliyah.com/lexicon.html.

Chapter 2

1. Strong's Concordance, "phaneros," #5318, www.eliyah.com/lexicon.html.

2. Strong's Concordance, "eidos," #1491, www.eliyah.com/lexicon.html.

3. Strong's Concordance, "grace," #5485, www.eliyah.com/lexicon.html.

4. Benny Hinn, *Good Morning Holy Spirit* (Nashville, TN: Thomas Nelson, 2004).

Chapter 3

1. Kenneth E. Hagin, *Plans, Purposes, and Pursuits* (Broken Arrow, OK: Faith Library Publications, 1988).

2. Rick Joyner, *The Final Quest* (Ft. Mill, SC: Morning Star Publishing Co.).

3. Strong's Concordance, "spoudaz," www.eliyah.com/lexicon.html.

Chapter 5

1. Strong's Concordance, "epiphanies," #2016, www.eliyah.com/lexicon.html.

2. T.L. Osborn, *Healing the Sick* (Tulsa, OK: Harrison House, 1986).

Chapter 6

1. Merriam Webster Online, "desecrate," merriam-webster.com.

Chapter 7

1. Strong's Concordance, "dexios," #1188, www.eliyah.com/lexicon.html.

2. Rick Joyner, *The Final Quest* (Ft. Mill, SC: Morning Star Publishing Co.), 140.

3. Ibid.

For more information about David E. Taylor
or to contact the author for speaking engagements visit
www.miraclesinamerica.org

Or call: 1-877-The-Glory
Missouri residents can call: 314-972-7926

In the right hands, This Book will Change Lives!

Most of the people who need this message will not be looking for this book. To change their lives, you need to put a copy of this book in their hands.

> *But others (seeds) fell into good ground, and brought forth fruit, some a hundred-fold, some sixty-fold, some thirty-fold* (Matthew 13:8).

Our ministry is constantly seeking methods to find the good ground, the people who need this anointed message to change their lives. Will you help us reach these people?

> *Remember this—a farmer who plants only a few seeds will get a small crop. But the one who plants generously will get a generous crop* (2 Corinthians 9:6).

EXTEND THIS MINISTRY BY SOWING
3 BOOKS, 5 BOOKS, 10 BOOKS, OR MORE TODAY,
AND BECOME A LIFE CHANGER!

Thank you,

Don Nori Sr., Publisher
Destiny Image
Since 1982

DESTINY IMAGE PUBLISHERS, INC.

*"Speaking to the Purposes of God for This Generation
and for the Generations to Come."*

VISIT OUR NEW SITE HOME AT
WWW.DESTINYIMAGE.COM

FREE SUBSCRIPTION TO DI NEWSLETTER

Receive free unpublished articles by top DI authors, exclusive

discounts, and free downloads from our best and newest books.

Visit www.destinyimage.com to subscribe.

Write to: Destiny Image
              P.O. Box 310
              Shippensburg, PA 17257-0310

Call: 1-800-722-6774

Email: orders@destinyimage.com

For a complete list of our titles or to place an order
online, visit www.destinyimage.com.

FIND US ON FACEBOOK OR FOLLOW US ON TWITTER.

www.facebook.com/destinyimage   facebook
www.twitter.com/destinyimage   twitter